Volume 5

MODERN FIGHTING AIRCRAFT

HARRIER

Published by Arco Publishing, Inc.

New York

A Salamander Book

Published by Arco Publishing Inc.,
215 Park Avenue South
New York, N.Y. 10003,
United States of America.

Salamander House,
27 Old Gloucester Street.
London WC1N 3AF,
United Kingdom.

ISBN 0-668-06069-7

Library of Congress Catalog Card
No. 83-83421

All correspondence concerning the content of this book should be addressed to Salamander Books Ltd.

This book may not be sold outside the United States of America and Canada.

Credits

Project Manager: Ray Bonds

Editor: Philip de Ste. Croix

Designer: Nick Buzzard

Diagrams: TIGA
(© Salamander Books Ltd.)

Three-views, cutaway drawings and color profiles: © Pilot Press Ltd. and Salamander Books Ltd.

Jacket: Steven Seymour

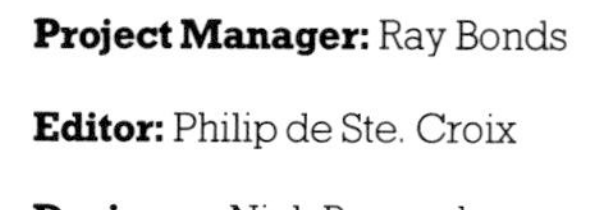

Acknowledgements

The author and editor would like to thank everyone who has contributed information and photographs for this book. Particular thanks are due to John W. Fozard, OBE, British Aerospace Divisional Marketing Director, who studied the text in meticulous detail. We are also grateful to John Godden, British Aerospace Aircraft Group, Kingston; Timothy J. Beecher, Lon O. Nordeen and Doree L. Martin of McDonnell Aircraft Co, St Louis; Geoffrey Norris and Karen Stubberfield of McDonnell Douglas Corporation (UK); David W. Hall, Rolls-Royce Marketing Manager for Pegasus and V/STOL and John Hutchinson, Rolls-Royce Ltd., Bristol; J. R. Ford of Ferranti plc; L. F. E. Coombs of Smiths Industries; and to the many people in MoD (RAF), MoD (RN) and the USMC who have assisted with the project.

Author

A former World War II RAF pilot and flying instructor, Bill Gunston has spent most of his working life accumulating a wealth of information on the history of aviation and military technology. Since leaving the service in 1948 he has acted as an advisor to several major aviation companies and become one of the most respected authors on scientific and aviation subjects as well as a frequent broadcaster. His numerous books include the Salamander titles *The Illustrated Encyclopedia of Modern Military Aircraft* and the *Aviation Fact File: F-111*.

A regular contributor to many leading international aviation and defence journals, he is a former technical editor of *Flight International* and technology editor of *Science Journal*. Among the many other authoritative journals for which he has carried out assignments are *Battle, Aeroplane Monthly, Aircraft* (Australia), *Aviation Magazine* (France), *Aerospace International, Aircraft Production, Flying, World Airways,* and the *Jounal of the Royal United Services Institute for Defence Studies.* He is an assistant compiler of *Jane's All the World's Aircraft* and has contributed to Brassey's *Annual and Defence Yearbook, Aircraft Annual* and Salamander's *The Soviet War Machine* and *The US War Machine*.

Filmset by SX Composing Ltd.

Color reproduction by Rodney Howe Ltd.

Printed in Belgium by Henri Proost et Cie.

Contents

Introduction

The story of the Harrier is without parallel. It began with a rather unwieldy scheme conceived by a Frenchman for vectoring jet thrust not only backwards, to achieve high forward speed, but also downwards, to make the aircraft rise vertically off the ground. Engine designers at Bristol translated the concept into a more elegant solution: a new type of aircraft engine able in one neat package to provide lift, thrust and even inflight braking. But the British, into whose lap the concept fell in 1957, had just been shortsighted enough to predict that the RAF was never going to need any more fighters or bombers. Future wars were going to be fought exclusively with missiles, which seemed a more attractive option because they were cheaper.

Despite these extraordinary circumstances, the completely new idea of a single-engined "jump jet" managed to survive. This was because American money paid for three-quarters of the engine, and one man – Sir Reginald Verdon Smith – said his company would pay for the remainder. A little later Sir Sydney Camm at Hawker Aircraft managed to persuade his board to pay for two prototypes of the novel P.1127 aircraft his team had designed. And in June 1960, four years from the start, British officials actually thawed enough to sponsor the P.1127 itself, provided that it was understood it was purely for research, and had nothing to do with such a taboo subject as a future combat aircraft!

With the passage of a complete decade, reason returned. The P.1127 was permitted to be turned into the Harrier, which gave the RAF the only kind of airpower that can survive in a future war, by being dispersed away from known airfields. It was also obvious that similar aircraft could completely transform airpower at sea, but, true to form, Britain put its foot in it a second time. Having, without actually announcing the fact, come round to recognizing that fighters and bombers were going to continue to exist, the government then pronounced that fixed-wing airpower in the Royal Navy was henceforth terminated, and that no more carriers would be built.

So we went through the charade a second time, permitting the development of the Sea Harrier provided that the ship to carry it was known by the strange title of "through-deck cruiser" (because to call it by the forbidden name "carrier" would have caused frightful ructions). Thus, by a second lot of back-door methods the Sea Harrier entered service, and so by the merest chance Britain was able to recover the Falkland Islands. Without the little jump jets the only response in April 1982 would have been to fume and bluster, and for the first time in modern history naked aggression would have paid off.

Where do we go from the Harrier and Sea Harrier? Why, on to the next generation, the AV-8B. This time the British government excelled itself. By announcing in 1975 that there was "not enough common ground" for a joint programme with the USA, Britain handed its birthright over to McDonnell Douglas. Now, freed from Whitehall at last, it will really go places.

The Jump Jet

In the mid-1950s the aeronautical world was becoming increasingly occupied with ideas for lifting fixed-wing aircraft vertically off the ground with the thrust of jet engines. For the next ten years every possible arrangement was studied, and more than 30 different schemes were actually flown. It is ironic that one of the least favoured of them should, after many years of fighting against not only the predictable ignorance, entrenched positions and totally closed minds, but also self-imposed political problems peculiar to Great Britain, eventually have won through to show the world that you can have airpower without either airfields or giant carriers.

Above: The pioneer free-flying jet VTOL device was the first Rolls-Royce TMR (thrust-measuring rig), popularly called The Flying Bedstead. The two Nene engines supplied air for four reaction control nozzles.

The self-imposed political problems stemmed from the now notorious *White Paper on Defence* of April 1957, which stated in the clearest terms that Britain's Royal Air Force was "unlikely to require" any more fighters or bombers – ever! Indeed, the phrase was interpreted in even stronger terms, to the extent that all combat aircraft programmes for the RAF were cancelled, excepting only the Lightning interceptor, which, said the Minister "has unfortunately gone too far to cancel". The very mention of future combat aircraft was enough to damage the career of officers or civil servants, and there was absolutely no point in anyone in the aircraft industry coming up with a new design.

It so happened that, just over a year earlier, Michel Wibault had put the finishing touches to a proposal for a combat aircraft unlike anything seen previously. One of the most famed French designers between the wars, Wibault had the vision to see that the numerous new NATO airfields being built in the 1950s might eventually become vulnerable to attack by nuclear missiles. Immovable, and littered with costly warplanes, they would present the ideal target. After much thought he came to the obvious conclusion: the only way to make airpower survivable is to divorce it from airfields.

Various VTOL (vertical takeoff and landing) aircraft already existed. Some were tail-sitters, pointing skywards, while others were flat-risers with swivelling engines or some other arrangement for obtaining both lift and thrust. Wibault devised a strange solution in which a gas turbine drove four large centrifugal compressors through gearboxes and shafts. Around each blower was a delivery casing – variously called a snail, a scroll, a diffuser or a volute – which could be rotated through 90°. With the four nozzles pointing downwards, the result was lift; with the nozzles facing rearwards, the result was thrust.

Wibault named his aircraft a Gyropter. He was not bothered about whether it should be a fighter or an attack aircraft; in the mid-1950s NATO was becoming interested in VTOL for both purposes. He was concerned with the basic principles, such as the need for the resultant VTOL lift force to pass through the aircraft CG (centre of gravity). He also knew that aircraft able to hover, a condition in which ordinary control surfaces are useless, have to have an extra control system using RCVs (reaction control valves) at the extremities, fed by compressed air. To drive his blowers he picked the Bristol Orion, with a sea-level potential of 8,000hp, as the most powerful turboshaft engine available, though the portly shape of his aircraft, and its relatively low-energy jets, precluded it from being supersonic.

Wibault failed to get much reaction from the Armée de l'Air or US Air Force, so he next took his proposal to the MWDP (Mutual Weapons Development Program) office in Paris. This was the agency through which a bountiful USA funded promising European military projects unsupported by their own nations. The MWDP director, Col Johnny Driscoll, USAF, was intrigued. Two years earlier he had supported the Bristol Orpheus, which was unwanted in Britain, and this had been the engine choice for all the contenders in the NATO light strike fighter competition, which was won by the Fiat G91. He asked the man behind the Orpheus, Bristol Aero-

Right: Typical of many free-flying rigs of the 1960s, this German VTOL helped in developing the VAK 191B strike fighter. Note the four RB162 lift jets, fed from two fuel drums amidships, and the wind anemometer!

Right: A Harrier GR.3 of RAF No 1(F) squadron recovers to its ship during Operation Corporate in spring 1982. It was the inherent simplicity of the single-engine vectored-thrust concept that enabled it to produce invaluable no-airfields airpower.

Engines technical director Stanley (later Sir Stanley) Hooker, to review Wibault's proposal. Hooker criticised the clumsy shafts, gearboxes, compressors and rotatable scrolls, but strongly favoured the use of a single engine for both lift and thrust, in a flat-rising jet. He showed the idea to his friend, the great Theodore von Kármán, who instantly said "Ah, vectored thrust" – today a common term.

Hooker took the scheme back to Bristol and handed it to his team: Charles Marchant, Gordon Lewis, Pierre Young and Neville Quinn. It did not take these brilliant young engineers long to come up with a scheme that retained the benefits while eliminating the drawbacks. Instead of bevel gears and transverse shafts to four blowers they proposed a single 1·5:1 reduction gear to drive two stages from the LP (low-pressure) compressor of the new Olympus BOl.21 turbojet, discharging through left and right vectoring nozzles. From this projected engine, the BE.48, further work gave the BE.52, in which the Orion was replaced by the lighter, simpler and cheaper Orpheus. Next, the BE.53 was produced by making the big front compressor an integral part of the engine, with a single front inlet, the inner part of its airflow going to supercharge the core engine and the outer part being discharged through the vectoring nozzles.

Fortunately Wibault was delighted at the transformation of his idea, and in December 1956 he and Lewis jointly applied for a patent for the first aircraft to look vaguely like a Harrier. This historic patent drawing not only showed two cold fan nozzles and two hot rear jet nozzles but it also featured contra-rotating spools and PCB (plenum-chamber burning). Making the HP (high-pressure) and LP spools rotate in opposite directions almost cancelled out the previously very large gyroscopic forces caused by the spinning masses in the engine, which in hovering flight would otherwise have caused severe problems. PCB is the vectored-thrust equivalent of afterburning or reheat, in that by burning extra fuel upstream of the cold and/or hot nozzles the thrust can be greatly increased for short periods. PCB was for the moment put on one side, to avoid its potentially thorny development problems. Without it the BE.53 would only give about 8,000lb (3630kg) thrust, but the immediate objective was to get something built and tested.

By great good fortune Driscoll's successor at MWDP, Col Willis (Bill) Chapman, was an enthusiast for VTOL. In the subsequent period of nearly 30 years the USAF has consistently stuck its head in the sand whenever it is asked what would happen if the many hundreds of Soviet missiles currently targeted on NATO airfields (including all those in the USA) were ever to be fired. In 1956, however, it was still possible to keep an open mind, and Chapman positively raced to find money to pay 75 per cent of the development bill of the BE.53. Equally quickly, Sir Reginald Verdon Smith, chairman of the Bristol Aeroplane Co (parent of the engine firm), agreed to finance the remainder, as he had done previously with the Orpheus. This was the crucial decision that got the whole project started.

Above: Seemingly perhaps the most attractive way to build a jet VTOL, the tilting-engine aircraft still poses many problems. Germany's VJ101C had six RB145 engines, two in the fuselage and two twin tip pods, and reached supersonic speed.

Below: When the Hawker P.1127 was being designed the only VTOL with official sponsorship in Britain was the Short SC.1, a slow five-RB108 aircraft (four for lift, one for thrust) which carried out a vast amount of fundamental research.

Hawker gets involved

Sadly, Wibault died at this juncture, and never saw his idea bear fruit. Another casualty was Maj Gerry Morel, brave French member of the British SOE who succumbed to his wartime treatment by the Gestapo and Vichy police. Director of the Société Franco-Britannique, he played a leading role in launching both the Orpheus and Pegasus, and as agent for Hawker he hosted Sir Sydney Camm at the 1957 Paris airshow just before he died. Camm said he had been watching the Rolls/Ministry VTOL schemes, with numerous special lift jets, with increasing disbelief. Morel asked him if he had seen the BE.53. On return to Kingston Camm sent a famous letter: "Dear Hooker, what are you doing about vertical takeoff engines?"

At the time Camm was immersed in trying to turn the Mach 2 P.1121 into the twin-engine, two-seat P.1129 to meet the TSR.2 requirement. Jet lift was a second-

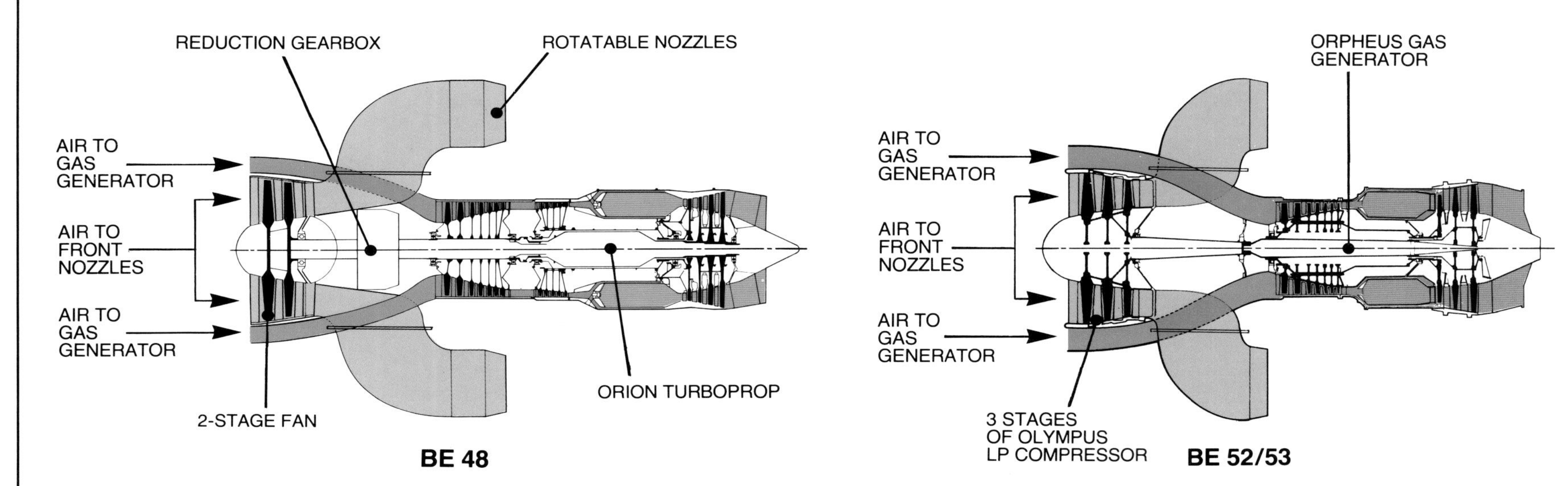

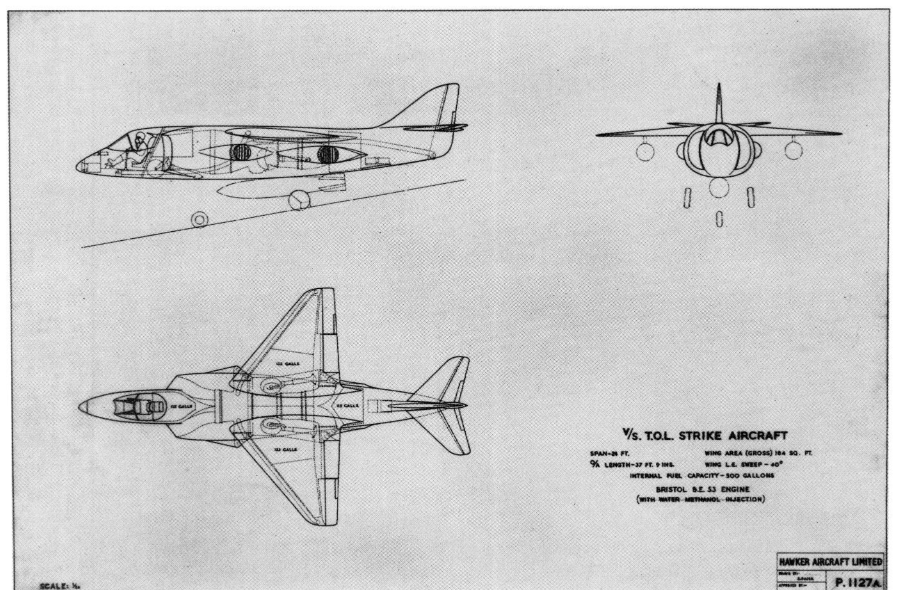

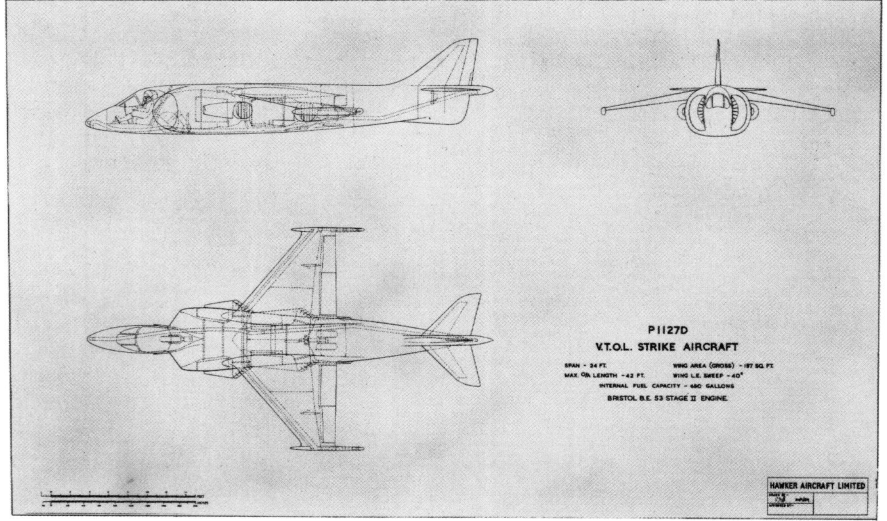

Top: An original company drawing from Kingston of the first of the P.1127 project studies. The words WITH WATER METHANOL INJECTION have been deleted by the designer. Note the conventional landing gear.

Above: The P.1127D was the aircraft actually built, and at company risk. This drawing, dated 20 September 1959, conforms closely to the first prototype, XP831, which began its hovering trials at Dunsfold in 1960.

ary matter, and in any case 8,000lb of lift from an engine based on the Orpheus seemed, in Camm's book, a typical engine-maker's overstatement. Hooker sent along the first BE.53 brochure, and Camm passed it to two of his best young engineers, Ralph Hooper and John Fozard. On 28 June 1957, in the same month as the Paris airshow, Hooper signed the first Hawker vectored-thrust drawing. As the jetpipe was not deflected, only the cold front jets were aligned with the CG, and the aircraft had to be STOL (short takeoff and landing), not VTOL. It was a rather slow three-seat battlefield surveillance aircraft. A little later it was refined into a two-seat support aircraft with lateral inlets. Meanwhile, down at Bristol the engine was developed into the BE.53/2, the first Pegasus, with mirror-image fan blading, to give contra-rotating spools to cancel out gyroscopic torques, and with the hot jetpipe bifurcated to a second pair of vectored nozzles.

Now the hare-brained scheme was suddenly looking plausible. As the P.1129 project became bleaker (because the RAF kept increasing the TSR.2 demands), so did the jet-lift work become more important. In August 1957 the first P.1127 brochure described a new aircraft designed around the Pegasus, with the four nozzles disposed around the CG under a high wing. This time it was a single-seater for attack and reconnaissance, and as it was a true VTOL it had air-bleed RCVs for control in hovering flight. Col Chapman was pleased with the proposal, but thought the range too short to be of real value to NATO air forces. Bristol raised the thrust to over 11,000lb (4990kg) by substituting the high-airflow HP compressor of the Orpheus 6, the result being the Pegasus 2. In early 1958 MWDP put up 75 per cent of the money for six of these engines, Bristol agreeing to pay the other 25 per cent, while Hawker Aircraft agreed to fund continued aircraft design and testing.

In the Pegasus 2 the engine had become a neat turbofan with the original bent pipe nozzles replaced by short nozzles with multiple cascade vanes to guide the flow. Bypass ratio was set at about 1·35, to match the thrusts from the cold and hot nozzles, and one major change was that the bleed power for the RCV nozzles was taken through stainless-steel pipes from the HP spool, Hooper having found that bleeding cooler fan air through aluminium pipes needed such enormous airflow that the pipes would not fit inside the wings! As there were only small gyroscopic effects, Camm was hopeful that complex triply-redundant three-axis autostabilization would not be needed. Hugh Conway, former managing director of Shorts and well up in the SC.1 autostab problems, later became managing director of Bristol Siddeley Engines. He gave a long briefing to Camm on what had to be done. After he had gone, the Hawker boss said "We are only ignorant buggers here at Kingston, and don't understand all that science. We'll leave the P.1127 simple, and let its pilots fly it".

The company-funded P.1127

The last major changes to the P.1127 were to adopt bicycle landing gear, with the wingtip outriggers made shorter by sharply sloping the wings down to 12° anhedral, the wing being placed above the fuselage so that it could be removed in order to change the engine. By mid-1958 Hawker Aircraft were busy testing models to investigate the novel airflows with sucking at the inlets and blowing at the four nozzles angled in various directions. In June 1958 the Ministry of Supply permitted tests to be done in government tunnels, and later extensive research was done at NASA in the United States, largely because the P.1127 was such an interesting aircraft. In March 1959 the Hawker Siddeley board boldly decided to fund two P.1127 prototypes, and work on these went ahead at high speed. By this time both the RAF and RN were daring once again to consider manned aircraft, including VTOL. Unfortunately, at the same time, Rolls-Royce, pushing its multiple lift-jet concept, announced collaboration with Dassault of France on a VTOL Mirage.

This seriously damaged the prospects of the P.1127. Having no home market, it was dependent on NATO, whose offices were already funding three-quarters of the vital engine. But the French made it clear they would have nothing to do with a British project, especially in view of Dassault's programme. To cut an extremely long and involved story short, while by April 1959 the RAF was at last openly thinking about a Hunter-replacement in the class of the P.1127, NATO had begun to plan a more ambitious scheme for a VTOL supersonic aircraft to meet NBMR-3 (NATO Basic Military Requirement 3). The latter resulted in a plethora of submissions from companies throughout the NATO aircraft industries, most of them as international collaborative projects. Hawker proposed a grossly stretched supersonic P.1127, the P.1150, powered by an uprated Pegasus with PCB.

NATO upgraded the NBMR-3 specification in its final form in March 1961, and the resulting Hawker submission was the P.1154 powered by the completely new Bristol Siddeley BS.100 engine of 33,000lb (14970kg) thrust. In April 1962 the P.1154 was declared the "technical winner" of the competition, but to appease France the rival Mirage IIIV was said to be "of equal merit". Moreover France predictably said it would never

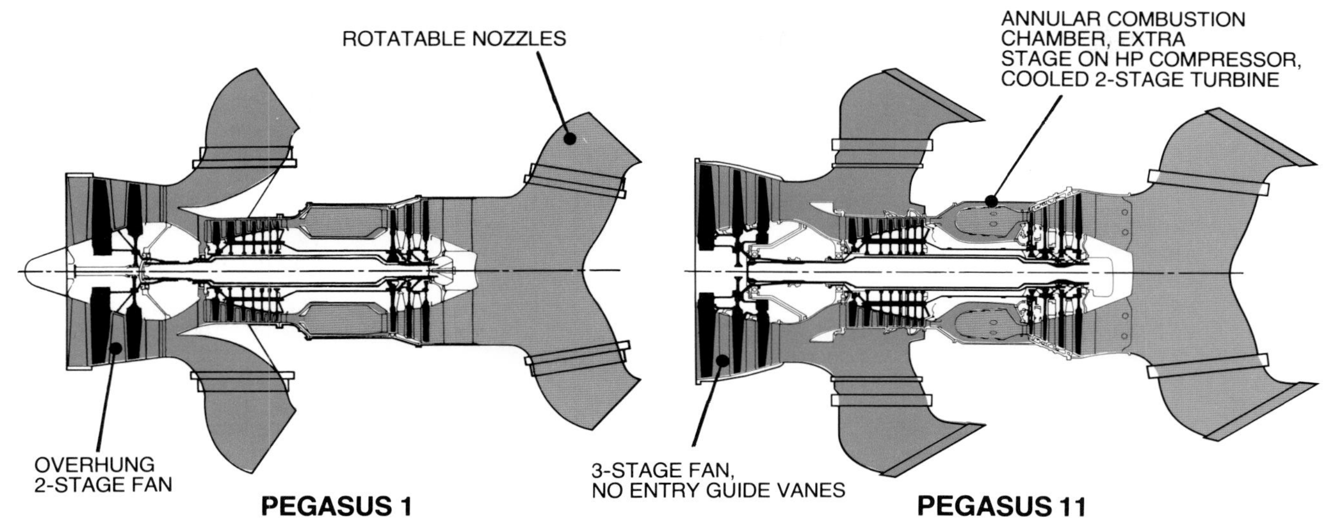

Evolution of the Pegasus

Simplified drawings showing how the first Wibault-derived scheme devised at Bristol, the BE.48, evolved over a decade into today's Harrier engine. The first two drawings, the BE.48 and 52/53, are slightly falsified in that the two inlets to the gas generator were actually at the top and bottom of the engine, while the front nozzles were on the sides. The significance of the colours is that magenta shows the hot portions of each engine, and blue the cooler elements. In today's Pegasus 11 the front nozzles discharge 110°C jets at 1,200ft/s (366m/s) and the rear 670°C jets at 1,800ft/s (549m/s).

accept any candidate but the Mirage IIIV, which it would continue to develop. This caused the whole NATO house of cards to collapse, and eventually the IIIV along with it, but it left both the RAF and RN looking for aircraft in the class of the P.1154. Eventually versions of the big supersonic Hawker aircraft were developed for both customers, but the RN did all it could to damage the programme by insisting on the maximum number of differences. Eventually the RN pulled out in February 1964, buying long-takeoff Phantoms (which it soon lost as the result of the 1965 decision to phase out British carriers). The RAF P.1154 was simply cancelled by the government in February 1965. The reasons were purely political, but, to explain the decision to the public, Prime Minister Wilson said that the P.1154 "will not be in service in time to serve as a Hunter replacement".

Below: The only serious rival to Hawker's V/STOL programme in the early 1960s was Dassault of France, which followed the Rolls-Royce formula (also supported by the British official establishment) in having a battery of separate lift engines. This was the first nine-engined Balzac.

More Phantoms were bought, which in fact cost more than the predicted P.1154 price and were available no sooner (and of course Hunters are still serving today in many air forces).

At the time, the cancellation of the P.1154 appeared a mistake of great magnitude, and certainly the decisions by the RN and the British government were taken for erroneous and very short-sighted reasons. Looking on the bright side, the British services were left with a nucleus of officers who understood a little about V/STOL, and industry was left with a wealth of experience. In any case, while the big supersonic V/STOLs were all the rage, the original Pegasus-powered subsonic programme had made great progress, though without any obvious eventual production application.

Bristol Siddeley Engines ran the first Pegasus 1 at Patchway in September 1959. Rated at 9,000lb (4082kg), this used LP bleed air for aircraft control and was for ground running only. The Pegasus 2 ran in February 1960, and at first all that Bristol could promise Kingston was 10,000 lb (4536kg). Hawker experimental pilot Hugh Merewether had been invited by NASA to fly the Bell X-14

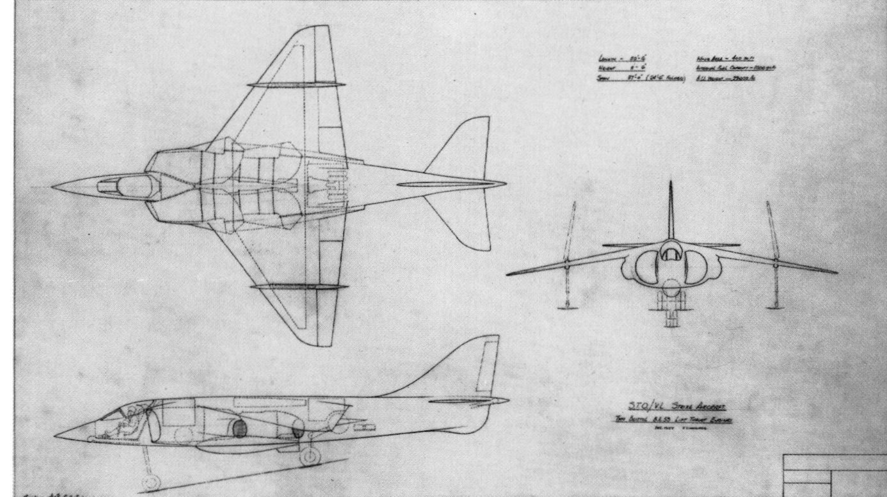

Above: Not previously illustrated, the Hawker P.1132 was an amazingly advanced aircraft for August 1958. It would have had two BE.53 engines, handed left and right to discharge on the outboard side of the engine only. Even at 1958 thrust ratings these would have allowed a gross weight of 29,000lb, the same as today's Harrier II, as well as transonic speed. This "STO/VL" was not built.

Below: Dated 30 September 1961, this drawing shows the P.1150/3 which was planned to meet the NATO NBMR-3 competition.

Bottom: The initial form of P.1154, which succeeded the P.1150/3 in the NBMR-3 contest. Later this impressive machine was further developed for the RAF, only to be cancelled in 1965.

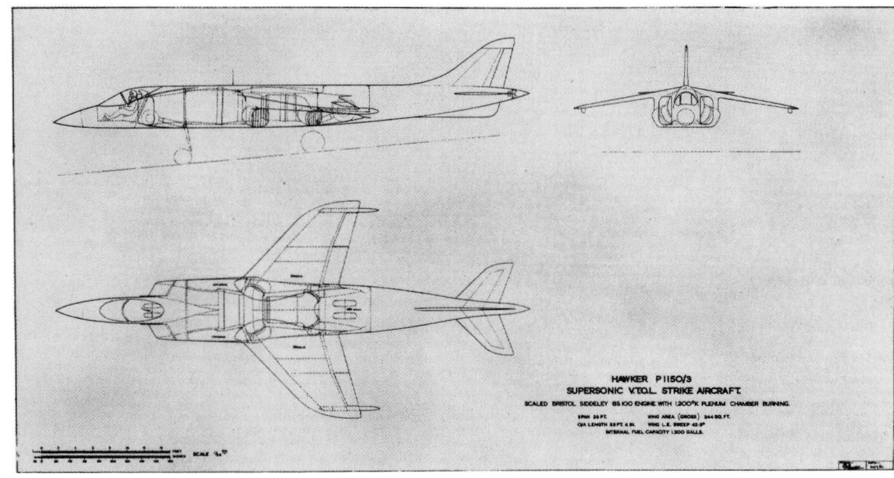

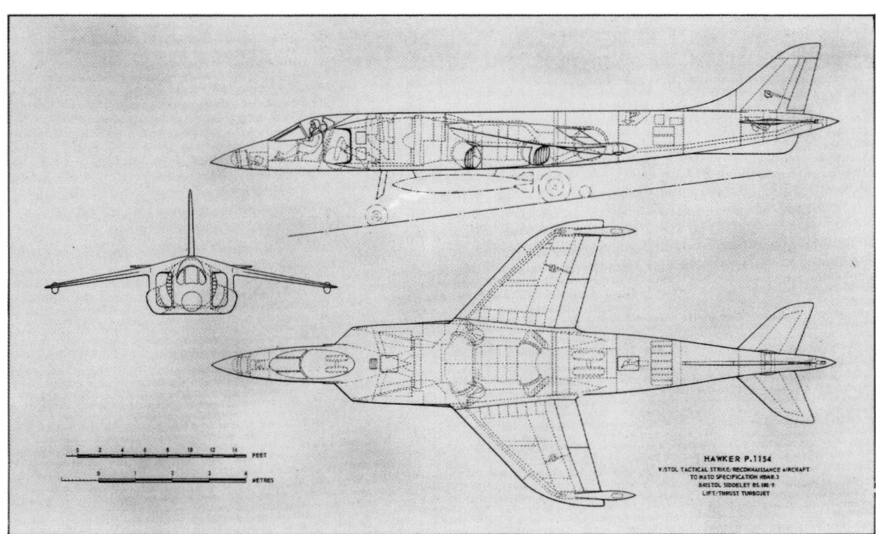

with vectored jets, and in making a vertical landing (VL) he ran out of roll power, even though both jets were at high power, and damaged the aircraft. Extra RCV power seemed a good idea for the P.1127, but it would mean even less thrust for lift, and Hawker's estimate of the first P.1127's empty weight was about the same as the promised engine thrust. Fortunately another 1,000lb (454kg) was then forthcoming from the installed engine, and in August 1960 it was cleared at 11,000lb (4990kg) for 30 min of VTOL or 20 hours of conventional flight.

By this time the two P.1127s were visible at Kingston, and to avoid embarrassment at having them emerge with no serial number the Ministry had at last coughed up some money in June 1960 and drafted a contract, both aircraft meeting experimental requirement ER.204D which was written around them. Serial numbers XP831 and 836 were allocated. Meanwhile, because the excess thrust for lift was so small, it was recognised that recirculation of hot efflux gas back into the engine inlets had to be avoided, so Hawker's airfield at Dunsfold was fitted with a special grid designed to channel gas well away from the aircraft. Hooker suggested to Camm that perhaps the first flight should be in the conventional (runway) mode, to check handling qualities. Camm snapped back "All Hawker aircraft have perfect handling qualities, the first flight will be a VTO"!

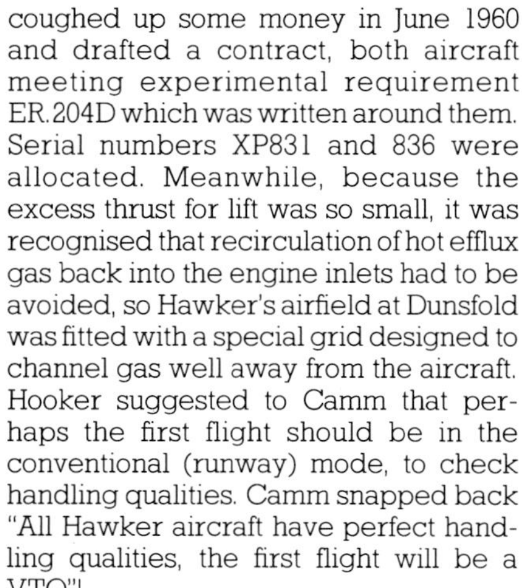

Testing begins

Ground running of XP831 began on 31 August 1960. Large bell-mouth inlets were fitted for these initial trials, and the aircraft carried the minimum of removable equipment. For hovering, in October, it was positioned over the grid with loose tethers to heavy weights. Even the wheel doors were removed, and the radio replaced by an intercom link. Chief test pilot A. W. "Bill" Bedford may even have wondered if the weight of plaster on his broken leg (gained as a car passenger in Switzerland) would prove the last straw, but on 21 October 1960 he got daylight under the wheels of the small prototype that was to lead to a new era in aviation.

There were problems, but also solutions. At rest the aircraft naturally tipped over on to one outrigger; always, on the next liftoff, there was inadequate RCV power with the Pegasus 2 to bring the wings level, so the aircraft would skid sideways across the grid and slew around in yaw. Again, inadequate RCV power made it impossible, even with full rudder, to stop the aircraft pirouetting tail-on to any wind, because of the powerful momentum drag in the inlets. And the tethers themselves caused great difficulty, so that Merewether said his task was "like trying to learn to ride a bike by riding down a narrow corridor".

On 19 November 1960 the hated tethers came off, and Bedford said it was "like freeing a bird from a cage". Free hovering proved most successful, and with progressive increases in engine thrust the missing removable items were replaced. A further improvement in RCV control came when, instead of having a swivelling rear pitch jet, the tail installation comprised separate pitch and yaw RCVs. But when high-speed taxi tests began it was found that the main gear hung lower than the outriggers, giving undue freedom in roll; poor nosewheel steering was combined with severe shimmy of the freely castoring outriggers, and the latter began leaving wavy lines of black molten rubber across the Dunsfold runway.

These problems were fixed by locking the outriggers and increasing their extension so that both touched the ground together. XP831 was sent to the RAE at Bedford, and after further high-speed runs Bill Bedford made the first conventional flight on 13 March 1961, far out-accelerating the chase Hunter. On 7 July 1961 the second aircraft opened its flight programme in the conventional mode from Dunsfold, and soon demonstrated speeds of well over 500 knots (576mph, 927km/h) at low level. By December 1961 this machine had gone on to pull 6g in sustained turns, reach over 40,000ft (12·2km) and achieve Mach 1·2 in a shallow dive. Then, because of a

Left: The first photograph of the first prototype P.1127, taken outside the Dunsfold hangar in August 1960 before the serial XP831 had been painted on. Later doors and other items were taken off to save weight

Below: Hawker Siddeley paid for this fully equipped ground-running pen long before there was any suggestion of Ministry funding. The picture was taken as the 2,000lb/sq in air bottles were starting the engine.

fault in the construction of the moulding, the glassfibre left front engine nozzle came off in the air. Bedford tried to land at RNAS Yeovilton, but when he lowered the flaps he entered a roll which could not be arrested, and he had to eject. A few days later a farmer arrived at Yeovilton with the missing nozzle, and though this facilitated diagnosis it took years before really satisfactory front nozzles were achieved. Eventually, though they do not really "need" such material, they were made of steel like the hot rear nozzles.

On the whole, flight development of the first two examples of this radical aircraft had been remarkably smooth, and there had been no need for any significant alteration to the aircraft or engine. This early phase was completed on 12 September 1961 by the achievement of complete transitions. Aircraft XP381 was either lifted off in VTO, accelerated forwards to high speed and then brought back to a VL, or taken off in the conventional mode, slowed in the air to the hover and then accelerated again for a rolling landing. In October 1961 operations were made from grass and other rough surfaces, and an especially important development was the start of STO trials, the nozzles being vectored down to 50° or 55° after a quick acceleration to about 60 knots.

In November 1960 the Ministry had funded four further P.1127s, actually calling these "development aircraft" as if they might be for something more than pure research. Soon there were plenty of detail differences as these came into use and, along with XP831, were progressively modified. Among the new features were a kinked wing leading edge giving increased chord at the tips, a row of upper-surface vortex generators to prevent wing drop at high Mach numbers, improved outrigger gears without pointed-nose fairings, Küchemann streamwise wingtips, modified tailplanes with greater area and 18° anhedral, improved RCV fairings and, for a time, inflatable rubber inlet lips that could be puffed up to a large radius for hovering and deflated to give a sharp lip for high-speed flight. Variable-radius inlets are needed for all jet V/STOLs, but a good scheme has never been devised. Rubber simply failed to stand up to high-speed flight.

Design improvements

Back in 1959 attitudes in the RAF and the Ministry had been changing. The TSR.2 project was well under way, and the Air Staff felt they could test the situation by writing a requirement for General Operational Requirement 345 for the simple Hunter replacement, which might well be a V/STOL. Though many officers scorned the P.1127 for its puny capability and lack of Mach 2 speed, some saw the possibility of future development. This obviously hinged upon what Hooker's team could do at Bristol, and they were already busy fitting the HP turbine with aircooled blades. This enabled gas temperature to jump from 977°C to 1,177°C, giving higher thrust. When combined with a new three-stage fan without inlet guide vanes, an annular combustor and other improvements, the result was the Pegasus 5, which soon gave 15,500lb (7030kg).

This at last enabled Hawker to design an improved P.1127 able to carry a little warload as well as fuel, but it is very doubtful that anything more would have happened – apart from the NATO fixation on much heavier supersonic V/STOLs – had not the United States come to the rescue a second time. Larry Levy, a wealthy American, had joined MWDP in Paris and had the vision to see that what was wanted was for NATO actually to get some service experience in, to see how jet V/STOLs could be operated in the field. He had the political clout to persuade the American, British and Federal German governments to fund a Tripartite Evaluation Squadron. Originally each nation was to put up the money and pilots for six aircraft, but – against German advice – this was cut to three on British pressure for economy. By early 1962 the RAF had given up GOR.345, and with it any hope of using a simple Pegasus-engined aircraft, deciding instead to go all out for Mach 2 with the P.1154. Despite this, the TES survived, because other nations were involved, and the aircraft were ordered by the newly created British Ministry of Aviation (formerly Ministry of Supply) on 21 May 1962.

The improved aircraft were called Kestrels. Powered by the Pegasus 5, they featured a new swept wing, with a thicker centre section causing a hump in the fuselage, which had first flown on XP984, the final P.1127. In its ultimate form this wing had small dogtooth discontinuities and extended-chord outer sections. A better relationship between the nozzles, wing and aircraft CG was obtained by splicing in extra fuselage sections above the front nozzles and below the rear nozzles (in effect moving the wing aft, as well as lengthening the

Right: Taken in 1964, this photograph shows the fifth P.1127 after it had received streamwise wingtips, inflatable inlet lips, eleven vortex generators on each wing, and the odd kinked-anhedral tailplane.

Flying controls

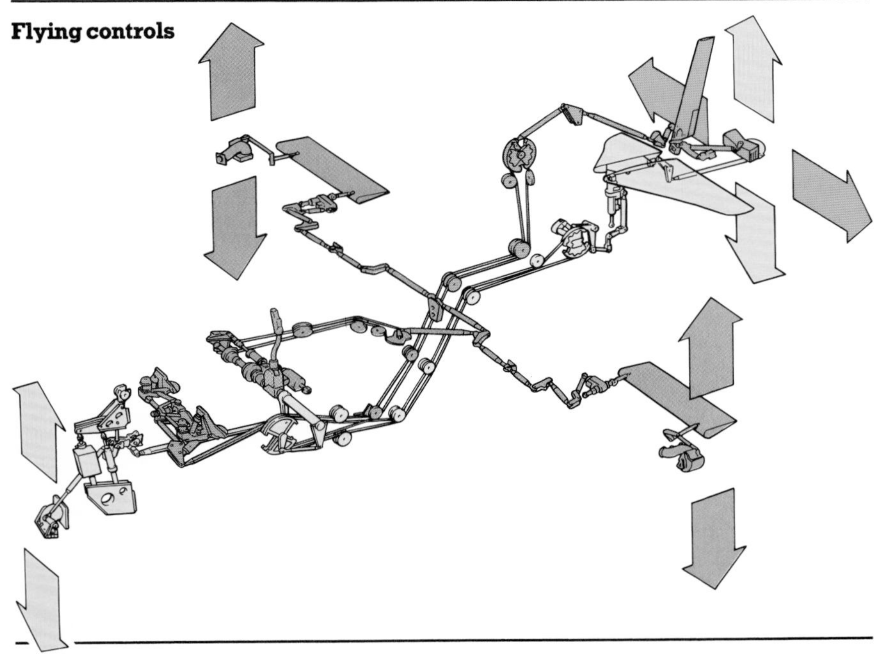

Left: If one had to put one's finger on a single aspect of the Harrier that has led to today's hard-won success it would surely be simplicity. Here the basic flight-control system is seen, and uniquely the normal stick and pedals operate not only the aerodynamic surfaces but also, and at all times, the RCVs (reaction control valves). As the engine nozzles are selected to angles at which powered lift becomes important, so do the RCVs come into effective operation, supplied with high-pressure engine bleed air to give thrust as shown by the large arrows. There is no change in control "feel".

Below: Not many photographs were taken of XP836, the second P.1127. This was chiefly because the glassfibre left front engine nozzle, clearly seen here, was made with an inherent structural weakness which led to nozzle separation in late 1961.

fuselage) and giving a sharper bifurcation to the jetpipe to move the hot nozzles forwards. By this time the hot nozzle fairings were all of the rectangular "spade" type instead of the "pen nib" type originally used, the flaps were extended in to the wing root, and toe-operated wheel brakes were standard. The Kestrels also had main-gear doors stressed for use as airbrakes, ventral strakes, taller fins, and eventually all had a substantially larger tailplane with a 16° anhedral and a kinked leading edge.

XS688, the first Kestrel but not quite up to full standard, flew on 7 March 1964. The TES was formed at Dunsfold under Wg Cdr D. McL. Scrimgeour, RAF, on 15 October 1964, and from April 1965 operated at RAF West Raynham and various unprepared dispersed sites in the neighbourhood. Its pilots were drawn from the RAF, Luftwaffe, USAF, USN and US Army. Two came from the latter service, though it had no hope of operating high-speed jets, whereas the Marines were not included despite their intense interest. The Kestrels had the pitot head on the fin, as in late P.1127s, and instead of a long nose probe a forward oblique camera was fitted. Under each wing was a pylon intended to carry a wide variety of stores, but these hardly ever carried anything during TES flying except 100gal (455lit) drop tanks, though on other occasions Kestrels dropped practice bombs.

Altogether 938 sorties were flown by the TES prior to disbandment in November 1965, roughly 24 missions per aircraft per month, with a total of some 600 hours. Takeoffs were made from concrete, tarmac, grass, compacted soil, various plastics and rubber sheets, aluminium sheet, glassfibre sheet, a portable pad constructed from interlocking aluminium planks, and plenty of surfaces covered with wartime PSP (pierced steel planking). Except for a US pilot who tried a rolling takeoff with the parking brake on, there was no serious incident, and the general opinion was extremely favourable. One of the most important benefits was that the TES got used to operating without a fixed airfield with centrally heated brick-built accommodation, which air forces had taken for granted since 1945.

Above: One of the first air-to-air pictures of the first Kestrel, taken in March 1964 with Dunsfold's Hunter T.7 two-seat chase aircraft in attendance. Rubber lips were fitted.

Below: Another view of the first Kestrel. This was still an immature combat aircraft, but apart from the engine designers, few knew what might later be derived from it.

Following TES use, six Kestrels went to the USA. By this time the USAF had decided it preferred airfields to V/STOL and chose to regard them as quaint foreign devices, despite their new US joint-service designation of XV-6A; according to *Aviation Week* it was "trying to think what to do with them". NASA, on the other hand, used XV-6As both at Dryden and at Langley for serious research, and found them valuable tools limited only by the 50-hour overhaul life on each engine.

This limited life was constantly being improved at Bristol, where, even if no funding had been forthcoming, Hooker's team would have kept on cranking in improvements. By early 1964, when no Kestrel had flown and all attention was focussed on the BS.100 engine for the P.1154, Bristol Siddeley was well advanced with a greatly improved Pegasus, the Mk 6, which first ran a year later. Its titanium fan handled substantially greater airflow, the combustion system was further improved with vaporizing burners and water-injection for short periods at enhanced power, both HP turbine stages were aircooled, two-vane hot nozzles were fitted, the fuel system was again revised and a life recorder was added. Despite its greatly increased thrust of 19,000 lb (8618kg), the Pegasus 6 was lifed at 300 hours.

The P.1127 (RAF)

This outstanding performance by the engine company, which had already more than doubled the thrust of the Pegasus with more yet to come, at last made it obvious that a Kestrel successor could fly useful combat missions. Though there continued to be factions within the

Left: Large grab-holds near the front nozzles identify this as an XV-6A, a Kestrel in the USA (actually aboard CV-62 USS *Independence*), seen in May 1966 during carefully measured carrier suitability evaluations.

RAF that scorned any Pegasus-powered subsonic aircraft, those who took the trouble to examine the possibilities came up with surprising results. Thanks to its economical engine even the Kestrel had demonstrated mission radius and endurance as good as the best Hunter, and with the Pegasus 6 it was possible to combine this with a war-load considerably greater than the Hunter could carry. In any case, V/STOL capability means that aircraft could be dispersed into front-line bases not only untargetable by missiles but also close to the enemy, thus enabling weapons to be carried in place of external fuel. It is fortunate that the CAS (Chief of the Air Staff), Sir Thomas Pike, took pains in 1962-3 to keep the Pegasus aircraft alive in parallel with the big BS.100-powered machines, and in 1963-5 his successor, Sir Charles Elworthy, did likewise.

When the Labour government took office in October 1964 it had campaigned partly on the fact that it would do away with British military aircraft. It informed the Air Staff that two of the three main programmes would be cancelled (later the third went, also). One of the first casualties was the P.1154. The Air Staff had seen this coming and began writing a new requirement, ASR.384, for a simple replacement for the Hunter in the tactical attack and reconnaissance roles, derived from the P.1127. The aircraft itself became known as the P.1127(RAF), but eventully was named Harrier, a name previously picked for the P.1154 and, back in 1927, for a Hawker bomber powered by an earlier Bristol engine, the Jupiter.

In a nutshell the proposal was that Hawker should produce an improved Kestrel powered by the Pegasus 6, and pack into it whatever avionic items from the P.1154 might fit. Even this fall-back proposition was only won with difficulty. Prime Minister Wilson, still professing to hate British planemakers, refused to sanction any suggestion of a possible production programme. The best deal the RAF could get was that the Ministry, which had just been renamed the Ministry of Technology (Mintech), would fund a small development batch. Then a decision would be taken on whether the P.1127(RAF) was worth putting into service.

Mintech came through with an order for six development aircraft, XV276-281, only two weeks later, on 19 February 1965. By this time Sir Sydney Camm had been Chief Designer for 40 years, and he had handed over the reins to John Fozard as Chief Designer P.1127(RAF). In 1966 Camm passed peacefully away on his local golf course, so like Mitchell with the Spitfire he never saw his last creation get into production. But for "Foz" and his design team it was a time of hectic action. Compared with the P.1154 the P.1127(RAF) was supposed to be easy, but it was not possible just to put the new engine and combat equipment into a Kestrel. Many parts of the airframe had to be redesigned, and it all had to be done in a very short time indeed, because first flight date had been fixed for 31 August 1966.

Left: The first military unit to fly the Harrier was No 1(F) squadron, RAF, which converted during 1969. This photograph shows a 1 Sqn GR.1 over the disputed territory of Belize, which this handful of aircraft have protected for over ten years.

The Harrier

When the "P.1127(RAF)" was at last allowed to be produced, after cancellation of the much more powerful P.1154(RAF), it bore the stigma of appearing superficially to be a second-best alternative. Because it was small and subsonic, many of the Air Staff still doubted that it would be of much real value, a belief heartily echoed by the USAF which by this time (1965) had ceased to show much interest in V/STOL because it could not see beyond supposed percentage penalties. It needed real dedication for the Hawker engineers to produce the Harrier right first time, and to a very challenging timescale.

Above: Completion of a NATO exercise in Norway, in temporary winter camouflage, highlights the way RAF Harriers have operated around the clock for 15 years.

While the P.1154 lived, nobody in the RAF was particularly interested in the smaller V/STOLs powered by the Pegasus. After the issue of ASR.384 and the contract for a development batch (DB) of six aircraft, the simplistic belief of many in high places was that the P.1127(RAF) already existed in the Kestrel; all that was needed was to install the Pegasus 6 engine and the extra equipment items that its power made possible. The team at Kingston knew better, but even they did not immediately realize that they would have virtually to start again with a different airframe. In fact, the redesign changed well over 90 per cent of the drawings.

Below: G-VSTO was a production Harrier GR.1, XV742, which in 1971 was painted in glossy epoxy camouflage and civil registration, with HSA logo on the fin. It was used as a demonstration aircraft pending completion of the company's own G-VTOL.

Airframe

For reasons already emphasized, the P.1127s and Kestrels had been made as light and simple as possible, but the P.1127(RAF) had to meet full service requirements. The structure had to be stressed to higher factors, the symmetric limit being 7·8g at maximum weight. The weights were all going to be considerably increased, yet the landing gear had to be stressed for more severe landings, with rates of descent to 12ft/s (about 3·66m/s). The entire airframe had to be designed for a safe life of 3,000 flight hours, to a most severe mission load spectrum, virtually all at very high speed at the lowest possible level, which meant demonstrating 15,000 hours on a specimen. Low-level jets suffer severely from the birdstrike problem, and though this mainly affected the inlet and engine it also meant the windscreen had to withstand the nominal 1lb (0·45kg) bird at 600 knots (1111km/h).

The wing managed to retain the original main structural box, which comprises two triangular boxes joined on the aircraft centreline. Upper and lower skins are machined from heavy plate to provide integral stiffening, and the inboard portion of the box on each side forms a sealed integral fuel tank, each of 172·5gal (784lit) capacity. The wing is tiny, because it was originally designed for high-speed flight, and low-level attack aircraft need the smallest possible wing in order to have minimum gust response, and thus give the pilot an acceptably smooth ride in rough air even at full throttle. Despite this small size, the extra lift of the wing on short rolling takeoffs is important in enabling more fuel or weapons to be carried, and later still the RAF took a leaf from the book of the US Marine Corps and studied the Harrier as an air-combat fighter, where a larger wing would show to advantage.

In any case, the wing differs greatly from that of the Kestrel. The section profile did not alter, remaining an NPL (National Physical Laboratory) "peaky" section with a generous nose radius, with thickness/chord ratio varying from 10 per cent at the root to 5 per cent at the tip. The leading edge was again redesigned, with extended chord outboard

Below: A Harrier GR.1 of RAF No 20 Sqn, shown with gun pods attached but otherwise in the clean configuration. Subsequently the appearance was markedly altered by the addition of the LRMTS on the nose and the RWR installation at the tail. No 20 Sqn later re-equipped with Jaguars.

Left: Taken in 1963, this picture shows the first Kestrel being built (the same aircraft is shown airborne on p.10). The integral-tank wing sits on the fuselage above the engine.

and initially a double kink leading to the inboard section; later this was replaced by a single dogtooth some way inboard of the inner small fence. Vortex generators were also needed. The Kestrel had finally had ten on each wing, but the Harrier began with four and ended with a row of 12.

Below: Slinging test at Dunsfold to demonstrate compliance with the requirement to hoist the aircraft with maximum fuel, weapon load, and pilot in the cockpit. If dropped from this height, the landing gear would absorb the energy.

More significant was the need to preserve longitudinal stability with full external stores, because this was before the CCV (control-configured vehicle) technology had matured sufficiently for an unstable fighter to be attempted. The specified stores loading was two pylons under each wing, rated at 1,200lb (544kg) inboard and 630lb (286kg) outboard. To retain adequate CG margins it was necessary to move the aerodynamic centre of the wing to the rear, and the obvious way to do this was to add area outboard. In fact, two tips were designed, both added immediately outboard of the outrigger gears. The normal tip can be unbolted and replaced by a larger tip giving extra span for improved cruising efficiency, and thus greater range for ferrying.

As before, the ailerons and plain flaps are of bonded aluminium honeycomb construction, both being hydraulically driven and the ailerons being positioned by Fairey powered flight-control units. Previously Fairey and Dowty had alternated for the contracts for the P.1127, Kestrel and P.1154. Despite Camm's dislike of clever devices, autostabilization was provided, but in a simple form with limited authority on pitch and roll only, without duplication. A light bobweight was added, and later the yaw axis was also brought in, but flight with autostab switched off is no problem. Hovering in gusty conditions is easier than with a helicopter, because the mean density of the Harrier exceeds 25lb/cu ft (400kg/m^3) and it needs little pilot input.

In solving the thorny problems of longitudinal control it was found that, aerodynamically, the final Kestrel tailplane shape could do the job, though with increased trim range. Structurally, it was back to the drawing board, because even with the Pegasus 5 the Kestrel tailplane had vibrated frighteningly during ground running, with jets aft, becoming a blur with 6in amplitude at a frequency of about 13Hz! To permit running with engine nozzles aft, the TES had had to anchor the tailplanes to the ground to meet the stipulated life of 1,000h. With the Harrier the required life was trebled, and engine power greatly increased, yet the final tailplane came out weighing 211lb (95·7kg), only 32lb (14·5kg) more than before. One of the many remarkable successes of Harrier flight development was to clear the aircraft with all combinations of external stores with impeccable handling up to AOA (angle of attack) exceeding 20°, despite the destabilizing effect of some 30,000 jet horsepower blasting a few inches beneath the tailplane.

Though closely related to that of the Kestrel, the fuselage was completely redesigned, with room for many extra items and stressed to much greater loads. A few items, such as Tacan and the nav/attack computer (avionics are described later), were fitted into the small nose, along with an F.95 oblique camera looking diagonally ahead on the left side. The seat became a Martin-Baker rocket-assisted H.9 or 9D, mounted on the sloping rear pressure bulkhead of the cockpit, which has the modest dP (pressure differential) of 3·5lb/sq in (24kPa). Though a flat front windscreen was required, for good view directly ahead, rear and aft vision were compromised by retaining a low--mounted seat and a canopy level with the top of the fuselage. There is a small rear-view mirror, but the view is limited both by the fuselage itself and the large inlets on each side. The canopy, opened manually along sloping tracks, contains MDC (miniature detonating cord) to shatter the acrylic moulding a split second prior to ejection.

The centre fuselage was restressed to carry two gun pods, as alternatives to belly strakes which, first used on the Kestrel, help to increase pressure on the undersurface in low-altitude hovering. In addition there is a centreline hardpoint for stores of up to 1,000lb (454kg). Two fuselage bulkheads, Nos 9 and 11, are stressed above the left inlet for a large oblique inflight-refuelling probe, which is attached on the rare occasions when it will be needed. Fuel is carried in five modest tanks, all integral with the structure: 51·5gal (234lit) each side aft of the inlets, 39gal (177lit) each side between the nozzles and 104gal (473lit) above the main-gear bay immediately behind the wing. Under the wing, immediately behind the engine, is the titanium drum containing 50gal (227lit) of demineralised water for injection into the engine combustor to restore thrust during VTOL operations on a hot day.

The rear fuselage was redesigned to house the main avionics bay and lox (liquid oxygen) container, with the associated air-conditioning bay immediately to the rear, served by a ram inlet in the base of the fin. The cockpit air-conditioning was located immediately behind the seat, in the space between the inlet ducts, with two projecting ram inlets in the dorsal surface and the system exhaust ejecting into the inner faces of the two inlet ducts.

Like other areas the inlets were again redesigned. Not only did the Pegasus 6 need a greater airflow, but this time there had to be a definitive inlet able to give acceptable efficiency at all speeds from flying tail-first up to over Mach 1, while at the same time withstanding severe birdstrikes on the inlet lip and on the curving wall which forms the inner skin of the forward tanks. By this time it was evident that the problems of any flexible variable-radius lip were not going to be solved quickly, if ever, so as well as reshaping the duct itself the problem of variable geometry focussed attention on metal mechanical systems. The final answer was a very short, sharply curved duct with a strong lip having the same peaky aerodynamic profile as the front of the wing, and provided with six suck-in auxiliary doors around the outside of each duct, mating with six more doors on the inner wall. The boundary-layer bleed slit on the inner wall, first used on the Kestrel, was enlarged and reprofiled to reduce drag and airflow distortion.

Unfortunately, no way could immediately be found to avoid distortion of the inlet airflow caused by the six auxiliary doors, which while admitting a large extra airflow caused cross-stream flow and turbulence and reduced pressure recovery. Further distortion was inevitably caused by the stream of hot air on the inner wall from the cockpit air-conditioning heat exchanger. While five of the six DB (development batch) aircraft had the inlet as described, a better configuration was eventually finalized after the DB drawings had been committed to manufacture. Thus, the production Harrier has a superior inlet system, outwardly distinguished by having eight large doors forming an almost continuous auxiliary-inlet ring. After flight development this system was made to behave almost perfectly over a range of inlet airflow angles and engine throttle rates equalled by very few other jet aircraft.

British Aerospace Harrier GR Mk 3 cutaway

1 Pitot head
2 Laser Ranger and Marked Target Seeker (LRMTS)
3 Windscreen washer reservoir
4 IFF aerial
5 Yaw vane
6 Windscreen wiper
7 Pilot's head-up-display (HUD)
8 Martin-Baker Mk 9D, zero-zero ejection seat
9 Boundary-layer air exhaust ducts
10 Cockpit air-conditioning system
11 Engine oil tank
12 Twin alternators
13 Engine accessory gearbox
14 Auxiliary power unit (APU)
15 Starboard wing pylons
16 Starboard wing integral fuel tank
17 Aileron power unit
18 Starboard navigation light
19 Roll control RCV (reaction control valve)
20 Outrigger wheel fairing
21 Starboard aileron
22 Hydraulic reservoir
23 Plain flap
24 Anti-collision light
25 Water tank
26 Water filler cap
27 Flap jack
28 Rear-fuselage fuel tank
29 Emergency ram-air turbine
30 Turbine release control
31 Equipment bay air-conditioning system
32 HF aerial tuner
33 HF notch aerial
34 Starboard all-moving tailplane
35 Rudder control linkage
36 Total-temperature probe
37 Forward radar warning receiver
38 VHF aerial
39 Rudder
40 Rudder trim tab
41 Yaw control RCV
42 Rear radar warning receiver
43 Pitch control RCV
44 Port all-moving tailplane
45 Tail bumper
46 Tailplane power unit
47 UHF aerial
48 Control system linkages
49 Twin batteries
50 Chaff and flare dispensers
51 Avionics equipment racks
52 Airbrake hydraulic jack
53 Liquid-oxygen converter
54 Hydraulic-system nitrogen pressurising bottle
55 Airbrake
56 Fuel jettison
57 Aileron hydraulic actuator
58 Port aileron
59 Aileron/roll RCV mechanical linkage
60 Hydraulic retraction jack
61 Outrigger wheel leg fairings
62 Port outrigger wheel
63 Roll RCV
64 Port navigation light
65 Bleed air ducting
66 Rocket pack
67 Outboard wing pylon
68 Aileron control linkage
69 Port wing integral fuel tank
70 1,000lb (454kg) GP bomb
71 Rear (hot stream) swivelling exhaust nozzle
72 Inboard wing pylons
73 Mainwheels
74 Pressure refuelling connection
75 Ammunition tank
76 Main undercarriage hydraulic jack
77 Fuselage flank fuel tank
78 30mm Aden cannon
79 Forward (fan air) swivelling exhaust nozzle
80 Engine monitoring and recording equipment
81 Ventral gun pod, port and starboard
82 Hydraulic-system ground connectors
83 Forward fuselage fuel tank
84 Rolls-Royce Pegasus Mk 103 vectoring-thrust turbofan
85 Supplementary air intake doors (free-floating)
86 Nosewheel
87 Landing/taxiing lamp
88 Nosewheel hydraulic jack
89 Hydraulic accumulator
90 Boundary-layer bleed air duct
91 Ejection-seat rocket pack
92 Engine throttle and nozzle control levers
93 Instrument panel
94 Control column
95 Rudder pedals
96 Pitch feel and trim actuators
97 Inertial platform
98 Pitch RCV
99 Camera port
100 Camera
101 Transponder
102 LRMTS protective "eyelids"

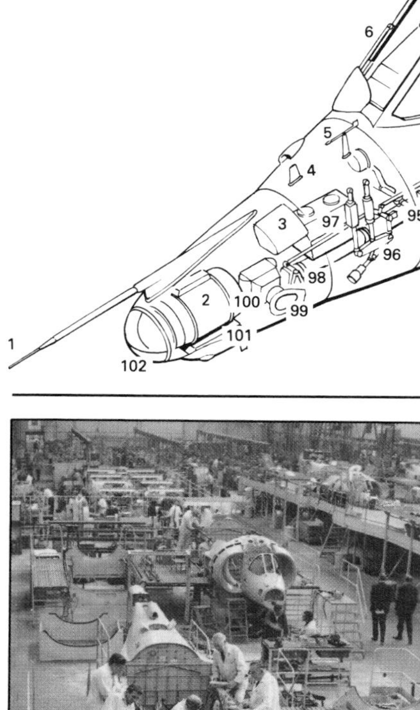

Above: AV-8A Harriers for the US Marine Corps on the line at Kingston in 1971. Because the wing is removed on each engine-change the fuselage and wing were virtually completed before the two came together at the flight-test airfield at Dunsfold, near Cranleigh, Surrey.

The last major development effort concerned the landing gear, which even in the Kestrel had been only passable rather than good. The primary objective of much greater energy absorption was met chiefly by increasing oleo stroke, without significantly increasing the loads to be absorbed at the attachments. Weak and spongy nosewheel steering was curable, but problems with excessive freedom in roll remained. In fact in early DB aircraft the heelover angle in turns worsened from 1·5° to 3·5°. The first of the six aircraft just made the due date, 31 August 1966, with a brief hover by Bill Bedford. Later, in fast runway operations, the unsatisfactory lateral stiffness on the ground became obvious, and in 1967 the decision was taken to redesign the main oleo into what was called the self-shortening form. On alighting, the new leg collapsed almost without resistance for the first 7·0in (178mm), by which time the outriggers were firmly on the ground. From that time on the landing gear, and all ground behaviour, has been better than that of most normal aircraft. Bay doors were arranged to close after extension of the gear to keep out foreign matter disturbed by the jets. Tyre pressures are typically 90lb/sq in (620kPa), or slightly higher for two-seat versions; this is fine for off-runway operations, and not much more than a quarter of the figure for the main gears of an F-15.

Powerplant

In many respects the Pegasus is unique. Conceived by Bristol Aero-Engines, developed by Bristol Siddeley and finally put into production after the takeover by Rolls-Royce, it is not only totally new in conception but it even broke much new ground in its basic design. The first time it was seen by the public it was doctored to resemble a conventional civil turbofan, the BS.58 (though bulges at the sides confirmed the rumours of vectored thrust with lateral nozzles), and even this looked novel with its inlet face completely devoid of any struts or inlet guide vanes (IGVs). Instead the front face of the engine comprised the first stage of the

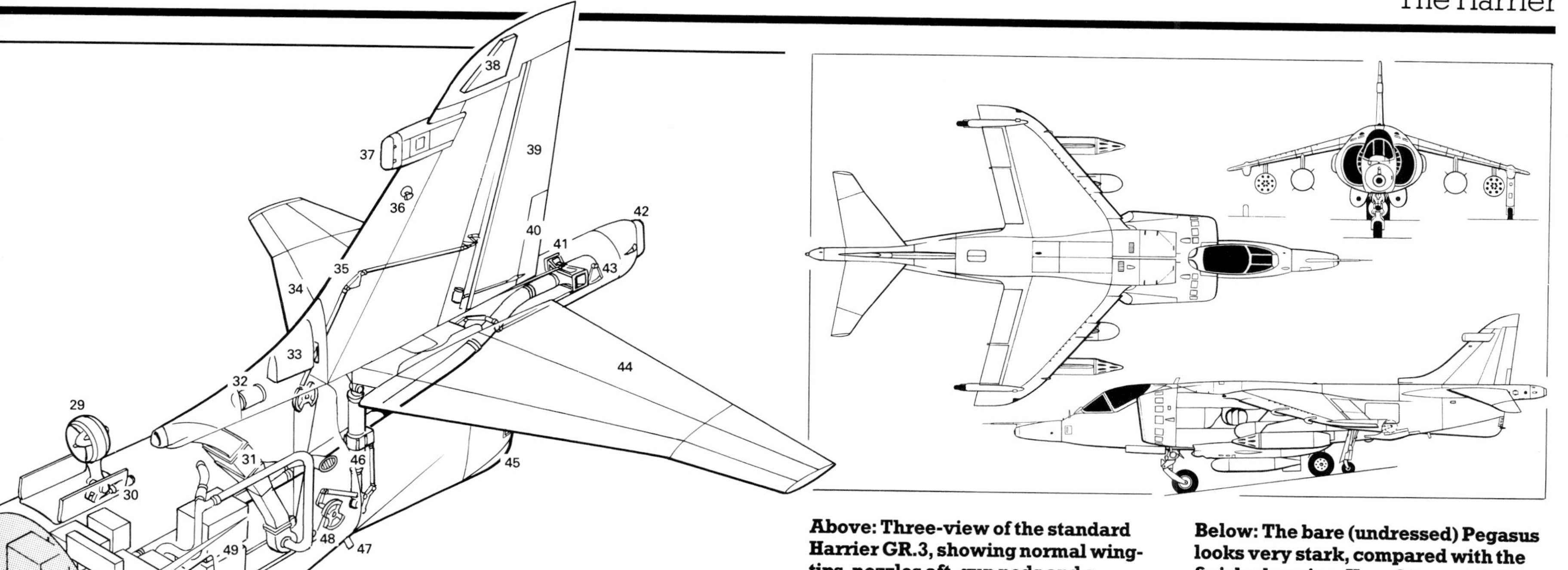

Above: Three-view of the standard Harrier GR.3, showing normal wing-tips, nozzles aft, gun pods and a representative ordnance load. The position of the retracted outrigger gear is shown by a broken line in the side elevation. LERX wing-root extensions flew on one GR.3.

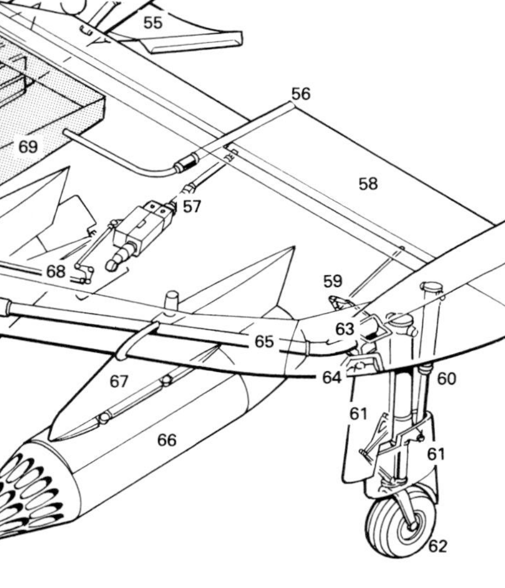

Above: Disposition of operational equipment in the Harrier GR.3, with shading showing the location of internal fuel. It is not yet possible to publish a similar illustration showing the Zeus active ECM system which is due in the late 1980s.

Below: The bare (undressed) Pegasus looks very stark, compared with the finished engine. Here fitters at Rolls-Royce Bristol are installing the GTS (gas-turbine starter) on top of the intermediate casing of a Pegasus 11 Mk 103 for a Harrier GR.3 of the RAF. Engine weight is 3,113lb (1412kg).

fan itself, though today most turbofans are built this way.

Dr Hooker's team were able to do away with IGVs because of the onward march of gas-turbine aerodynamics. IGVs had been needed in earlier engines to swirl the incoming air in the direction of rotation of the moving blades downstream, in order that the Mach number of the flow past the outer parts of the blades should always be well below 1. The development of thin, sharp-edged blades of so-called lenticular form enabled Mach number at the tips to go well into the supersonic region, up to about 1·5. Once the flow was supersonic, there was no point in having IGVs. Their omission saved engine length, weight and cost, improved resistance to bird-strikes and made it possible to eliminate all inlet anti-icing systems.

A further innovation, bold at the time but today commonplace, was to make the entire fan overhung, in other words to cantilever it ahead of the front bearing. The fan's light weight, large diameter and enormous airflow made vibration a problem, and there was bound to be severe vibration because of the extremely short inlet ducts, which in turn stemmed from the fact the engine had to be centred around the aircraft CG. The main resonant blade frequencies thus had to be kept outside the running speed range, and this was achieved by fitting snubbers (mid-span shrouds) to the blades, so that they all touched each other. This also solved the problem of distortion of static pressure distribution downstream of the fan, where it discharges into a plenum chamber which feeds the two front nozzles. The production engine has three stages of fan blades, all made in Hylite 45 titanium alloy in place of the Pegasus 3's aluminium, and all with snubbers.

In the same way, the need to split the hot gas downstream of the turbines and discharge it through left and right nozzles demanded a sharply bent exhaust duct, and this induced vibration in the LP turbine blades. The method of attack was rather similar, in that all blades in the second HP and both LP stages were drilled near mid-span and heat-resistant wire laced through to give an anti-vibration link joining all blades in each stage. (Today, in the AV-8B, new shrouded LP blades are used instead, avoiding the loss in efficiency of the gas flowing past the wires.)

There are many other technically interesting parts of the Pegasus, including the combustion system which, in sharp contrast to the original Orion and Orpheus, has a fully annular chamber with vaporizing burners. The latter were among the technologies inherited when Armstrong Siddeley joined Bristol to form Bristol Siddeley, and after careful tests the Bristol team were not too proud to admit that the Coventry firm's idea was superior. As a result the Harrier's combustion has generally been perfection, and its absence of visible smoke adds to its elusiveness which is a great bonus in warfare.

All other aspects of the Pegasus, however, pale into insignificance compared with the underlying need to vector the entire engine thrust through 98·5°. No other engine of such power has ever been thus vectored, nor fitted with four nozzles. It was clear from the start that the four nozzles simply *had* to move in unison, in the same way that the wings have to stay fixed to the fuselage. Moreover, with thrust often much greater than the total weight of the aircraft, the angles of the nozzles had to be controlled accurately. Thus, all four nozzles had to move together and, in any setting, all four had to be positively locked.

The final scheme adopted is to bleed HP air, the same 400°C supply as that fed to the RCVs, and use it to power two motors driving a differential gearbox in such a way that, if either motor jams, the other continues to drive but at half-speed. From this gearbox the scheme echoes the Wibault concept, in that a drive shaft along the underside of the engine is geared to two cross shafts. Instead of then using further gears, Hooker wisely elected to use chains. The chain drives have proved to be totally reliable, light and free from backlash or other problems. Credit for the air servo-motor goes to the Plessey company, though the entire system was produced by Hawker. It is controlled by a single lever in the cockpit, which is the only control in the Harrier cockpit not found on normal aircraft. It can drive the nozzles at rates up to 100°/s. As explained later, the system eventually matured as an extra flight trajectory control for use in air combat.

Systems

The flight control system in a V/STOL aircraft really has to comprise two systems, one for use in V/STOL flight and the other, the conventional system, for use only at speeds sufficiently high for

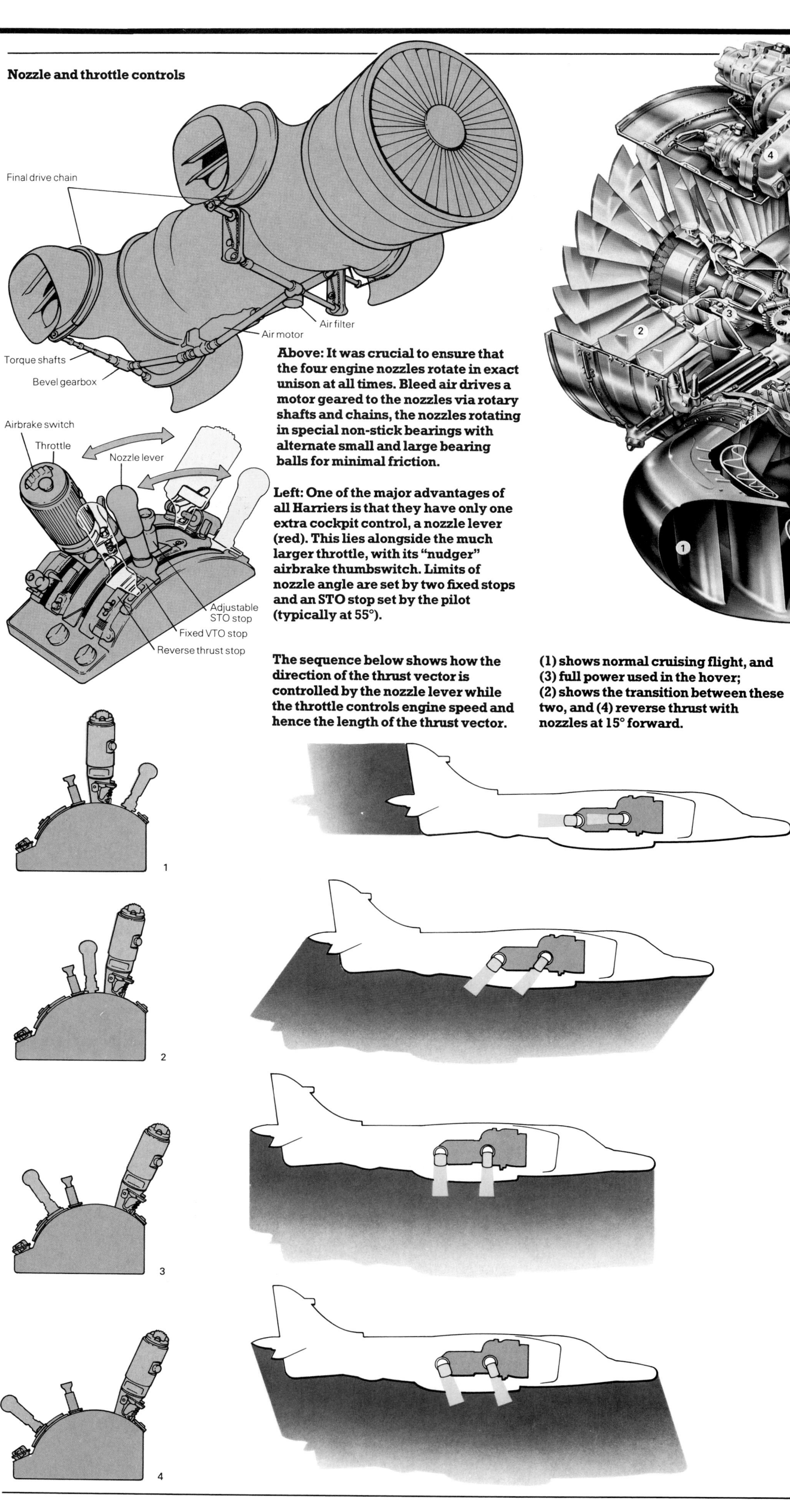

Above: It was crucial to ensure that the four engine nozzles rotate in exact unison at all times. Bleed air drives a motor geared to the nozzles via rotary shafts and chains, the nozzles rotating in special non-stick bearings with alternate small and large bearing balls for minimal friction.

Left: One of the major advantages of all Harriers is that they have only one extra cockpit control, a nozzle lever (red). This lies alongside the much larger throttle, with its "nudger" airbrake thumbswitch. Limits of nozzle angle are set by two fixed stops and an STO stop set by the pilot (typically at 55°).

The sequence below shows how the direction of the thrust vector is controlled by the nozzle lever while the throttle controls engine speed and hence the length of the thrust vector. (1) shows normal cruising flight, and (3) full power used in the hover; (2) shows the transition between these two, and (4) reverse thrust with nozzles at 15° forward.

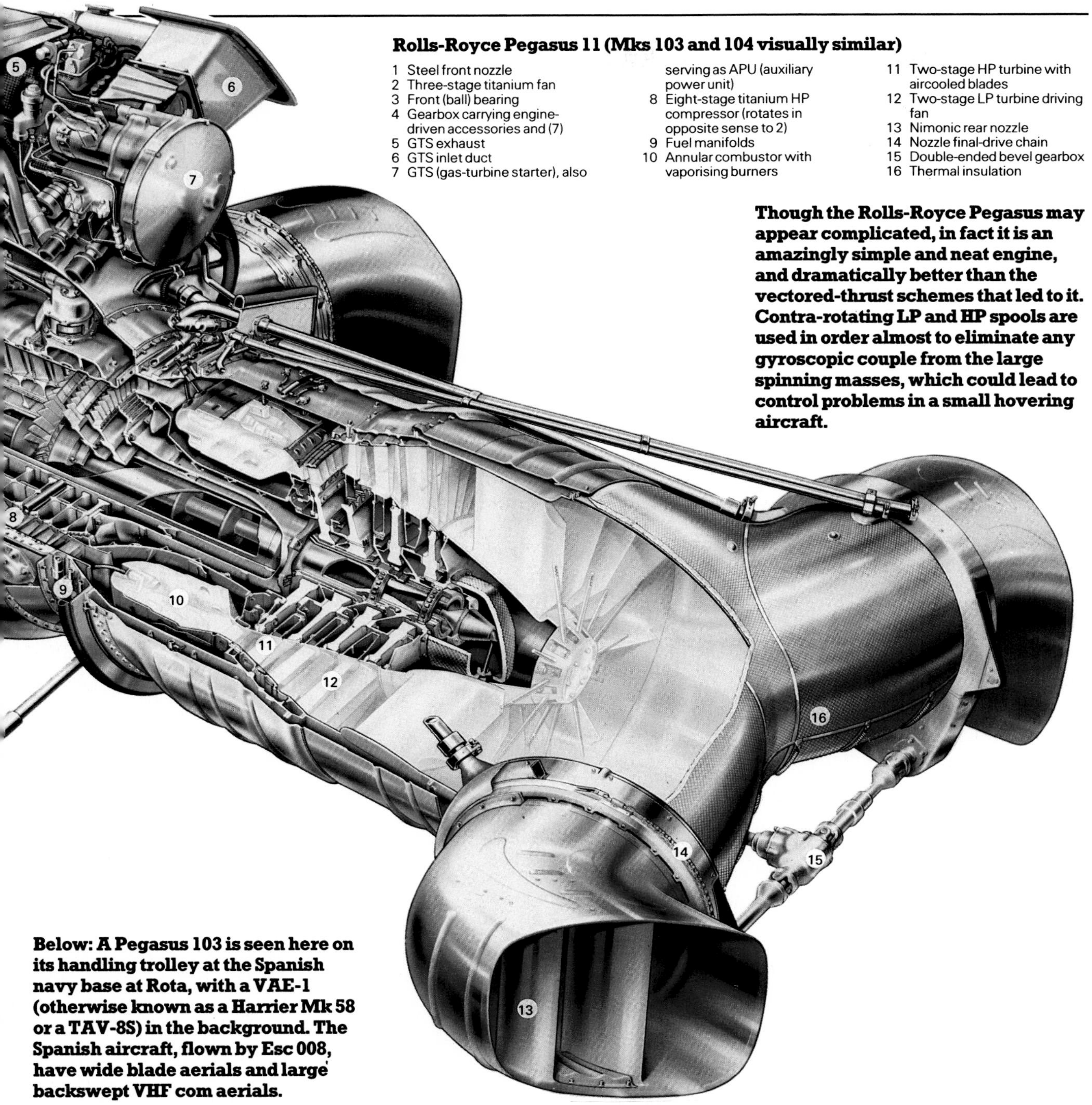

Rolls-Royce Pegasus 11 (Mks 103 and 104 visually similar)

1 Steel front nozzle
2 Three-stage titanium fan
3 Front (ball) bearing
4 Gearbox carrying engine-driven accessories and (7)
5 GTS exhaust
6 GTS inlet duct
7 GTS (gas-turbine starter), also serving as APU (auxiliary power unit)
8 Eight-stage titanium HP compressor (rotates in opposite sense to 2)
9 Fuel manifolds
10 Annular combustor with vaporising burners
11 Two-stage HP turbine with aircooled blades
12 Two-stage LP turbine driving fan
13 Nimonic rear nozzle
14 Nozzle final-drive chain
15 Double-ended bevel gearbox
16 Thermal insulation

Though the Rolls-Royce Pegasus may appear complicated, in fact it is an amazingly simple and neat engine, and dramatically better than the vectored-thrust schemes that led to it. Contra-rotating LP and HP spools are used in order almost to eliminate any gyroscopic couple from the large spinning masses, which could lead to control problems in a small hovering aircraft.

Below: A Pegasus 103 is seen here on its handling trolley at the Spanish navy base at Rota, with a VAE-1 (otherwise known as a Harrier Mk 58 or a TAV-8S) in the background. The Spanish aircraft, flown by Esc 008, have wide blade aerials and large backswept VHF com aerials.

ordinary control surfaces to be effective. As already noted, the conventional system is fully powered and irreversible, apart from the rudder which has a trim tab and manual drive. The horizontal tail is made up of left and right "slabs" without elevators, and it resembles that of the F-4 Phantom in having a large angular movement and marked anhedral. Roll is controlled solely by the small ailerons, though partly because of the short span the rates of roll are good.

At low speeds and in hovering flight the RCV system is progressively energized. There is no sudden transfer from one system to the other; the aerodynamic surfaces continue to be deflected, but as speed is reduced down to the hover, so does the RCV system progressively and smoothly take over. The linkages to the RCV system are, in fact, driven from the local conventional flight-control circuits. The ailerons drive roll RCVs at the front of the outrigger gear fairings. The rudder drives the yaw RCV in the projecting tail end of the fuselage. The tailplane drives the nose-down pitch RCV at the tail, while the nose-up RCV under the nose is driven directly from the stick.

The RCV system is not brought in by q-feel (dynamic pitot pressure) or an airspeed sensor, but simply according to the position of the main engine nozzles. When the nozzles are fully aft, the master shut-off valve under the engine HP compressor delivery is closed; thus, though pilot flight-control demands move both the aerodynamic surfaces and the RCVs, the latter's shutters open and close without any compressed air emerging. As soon as the engine nozzles move away from the fully aft position, the master shut-off valve begins to open. Rapidly the supply pressure in the stainless-steel pipes builds up until, when the engine nozzles are at about 20°, the master valve is fully open. Pilot control demands now result in the aerodynamic surfaces being accompanied by extremely powerful blasts from the associated RCVs.

It might not be appreciated just how powerful the RCV system has to be. The air supply is at 400°C (750°F), almost a dull-red temperature, and at a nozzle exit pressure of 150lb/sq in (1034kPa). The RCVs are heat-resistant steel, with convergent nozzles opened or closed by shutters sealed by sliding carbon bearings. In action, each RCV emits a supersonic jet moving at about 1,700mph (2740km/h). At full control demand the Harrier RCV system is transmitting energy at a rate of several thousand horsepower.

The early P.1127s had a constant-bleed system for the RCVs, and pilot demands merely shut down some valves and opened others wider. Such a system would be unacceptable in the Harrier, for the loss in available engine thrust would be serious, quite apart from denuding the engine turbines of air pumped by the compressor, thus increasing gas temperature. The Harrier instead has a demand system. When the pilot's cockpit controls are centred, no air is consumed. Stick and rudder movements open the appropriate RCVs progressively, to give a smooth and natural aircraft response. Particular effort was needed to perfect the roll RCVs, and achieve exactly the right "gearing", in terms of matching roll response to pilot stick deflection. The roll RCVs are especially interesting in that each is cunningly made to blast air either upwards or downwards, depending on the pilot demand, thus doubling the roll control power in comparison with that from a unidirectional RCV installation.

Most secondary power functions in the Harrier are served by the hydraulic system. This is duplicated, energized by two engine-driven pumps to a pressure of 3,000lb/sq in (20.69MPa). It serves the flying control system, flaps, landing gear and doors (the latter closing with gear down), airbrake, adaptive anti-skid wheel brakes, windscreen wiper and the jack which extends the RAT (ram-air turbine). The latter, normally retracted in a box in the top of the rear fuselage, can be extended to provide emergency system pressure. It provides ample power for flight control, but in view of the special nature of the Harrier, and the demanding nature of a dead-stick (engine off) landing, the RAT is being removed from RAF Harriers. In emergency, hydraulic items can be moved by stored nitrogen pressure.

Electrical power is generated as AC (alternating current) by two 12kVA alternators projecting ahead of the accessory gearbox above the engine fan case. TRUs (transformer/rectifier units) convert some power to DC, part of which charges the two batteries. The latter, in the rear fuselage, provide power to start a Lucas gas-turbine APU (auxiliary power unit), which is mounted on the rear of the accessory gearbox where it fits above the Pegasus plenum chamber. It can be started from the cockpit in the most extreme climatic conditions, and makes the Harrier completely independent of any ground power. Among other things it drives a 6kVA alternator for ground servicing and stand-by, and also serves as the starter for the Pegasus. The APU draws in air from a rectangular inlet in the top of the fuselage and discharges exhaust from a second flush aperture nearby.

Pilot oxygen is supplied from a Normalair-Garrett lox converter of 1gal (4·5lit) capacity. Like other system components, this is located in the rear fuselage, in this case immediately above the airbrake.

Fuel tankage in the airframe has been described, and it can be supplemented by two drop tanks carried on the "wet" (plumbed) inboard wing pylons. Originally the Harrier was cleared with combat tanks of 100gal (455lit) or ferry tanks of 330gal (1500lit), the latter seldom being needed in European service. During Operation Corporate (see later chapter) new tanks of 190gal (864lit) size were also flown, though these are not used by the RAF. The ground pressure-fuelling connection is immediately ahead of the left rear engine nozzle. The flight-refuelling probe, roughly 10ft (3m) in length, is attached above the left inlet and coupled to the inflight-refuelling valve in the aircraft fuel system. The probe is inclined upwards and outwards so that its tip is easily visible to the pilot. Finally, the large airflow and power of the Pegasus tend to give a false idea of the Harrier's fuel consumption. In the worst condition, hovering at full weight at sea level, fuel burn is 220lb (100kg)/min. This is one-sixth that of an F-4 Phantom on take-off.

Avionics

When the P.1127(RAF) was rather suddenly invented, upon cancellation of the P.1154(RAF), there was no background of an RAF OR (operational requirement) or official specification. As time was pressing, the Air Staff merely issued ASR.384 as a re-issue of the most recent

Right: Taken during an actual RAF low-level training sortie, this photograph shows how the pilot can look simultaneously both at the HUD display and at the scene ahead. The Harrier is diving into the valley.

Above: The cockpit of an RAF GR.3, showing the traditional dial instruments. The HUD and head-down moving-map display are on the centre-line; left are flight instruments with the weapon panel below.

Harrier GR.3 Cockpit Layout

1 Pilot display unit
2 Flying instruments
3 PDU controls
4 Weapon control panel
5 V/UHF controls
6 Throttle and nozzle box
7 Hand controller
8 F.E. 541 NDC (navigation display computer) unit
9 Engine instruments
10 Fuel instruments
11 F.E. 541 NDC control
12 Centralised warning system panel
13 Tacan controls
14 Voice recorder
15 IFF (identification friend or foe) controls

Left: Though well-known, this is still the best photograph yet taken of SNEB rockets being fired from an RAF Harrier. This Ministry of Defence (RAF) picture dates from GR.1 days. The photographer was looking almost straight up at the diving aircraft, firing on a ground target.

draft of OR.356, which was the document covering the P.1154(RAF), but with the radar omitted and the mission numbers down-graded to suit the anticipated mission capability of the smaller, subsonic Pegasus-powered aircraft.

The radar was omitted because it would have been extremely difficult to include it, there was no mention in ASR.384 of air combat missions, and the equipment itself did not yet exist (the supplier, Ferranti, had not even been awarded the full development contract). Apart from this item, much of the P.1154(RAF) avionics suite was written in without change, notably including the INAS, HUD and NDC.

The INAS (inertial navigation attack system) is the Ferranti FE.541, which because of its NBMR-3 application was actually designed for the P.1154(RAF). Its basis is the inertial platform in the nose, bolted to the cockpit front pressure bulkhead, which feeds positional information to the IMS (inertial measurement system) and present-position computer, which in turn feeds position information to the NDC (navigation display computer) and trajectory information to the WAC (weapon-aiming computer). The NDC is also called a projected map display, because its main display is a circular screen on which is projected optically a 35mm cassette containing a selected topographic map covering typically 800nm (921 miles, 1483km) north/south and 900nm (1,036 miles, 1668km) east/west.

There are two other inputs to the NDC. One is traditional Tacan, the long-established radio navaid which gives R-theta (radius and bearing) information from an interrogated ground station. The other is the Sperry C2G gyrocompass, providing an additional source of heading information. Present position is at the centre of the NDC, and the pilot himself has inputs in the form of buttons on the NDC, and a separate pistol-grip hand controller with a rolling-ball input and white "fix" button, which is depressed as the aircraft overflies a point whose position must be recalled or which must later be regained.

The third major avionic item specified at the start was the HUD (head-up display). This was designed by a small firm called Specto, which was taken over by Smiths Industries. It receives height and speed information from the ADC (air-data computer) and cockpit HUD control panel (and, after this item had been fitted, the LRMTS, as described in the next chapter). The HUD provides basic flight guidance information for all modes of flight, including a vital cue showing any tendency to sideslip at speeds too low for natural weathercocking by the fin, as well as the primary steering information for all air-to-ground or air-to-air attacks.

A HUD camera was specified to record the display as a training aid, and other basic avionics included HF, VHF and UHF radio, and IFF (identification friend or foe). Tactical VHF was also called for, but in fact this was never fitted until it appeared on AV-8 series aircraft of the US Marines and Spanish Navy.

After delivery, two very important extra items changed the appearance of Harriers of the RAF. These, the LRMTS and RWR, are described in the next chapter. EW (electronic-warfare) installations are also discussed there, and in the account of Operation Corporate.

Weapons

No internal weapons were called for. Like the P.1154(RAF) the Harrier was to rely solely on externally carried stores, though the supersonic predecessor's emphasis on guided missiles (such as Red Top and AS.30) was replaced by simpler weapons thought more appropriate to a tactical battlefield situation: bombs, rocket pods, and external gun pods. Hawker designed the pods to accommodate a single Aden Mk 4 gun of 30mm calibre together with its ammunition. The ammunition box accommodates 100 rounds, and 130 can be accommodated without causing feed problems if the capacity of the feed chutes is utilized. For minimum aircraft drag the firing aperture at the front of the pod is covered by a frangible cap, blown off by the first round. These pods have a useful effect as LIDs (lift-improvement devices), and when removed are replaced by thin strakes serving the same purpose.

Details of weapon loads are given in a diagram. The maximum weight of external loads can reach 9,000lb (4082kg), but the limit for normal operations is 5,300lb (2400kg). For the reconnaissance mission, the centreline fuselage pylon can carry a Hawker pod housing five optical cameras, two left and two right oblique F.95 Mk 7s and a forward F.135. Since the Falklands campaign RAF Harriers have carried AIM-9 Sidewinder self-defence AAMs.

Below: Selected weapons carried by the RAF and US Marine Corps, the American stores being in brackets.

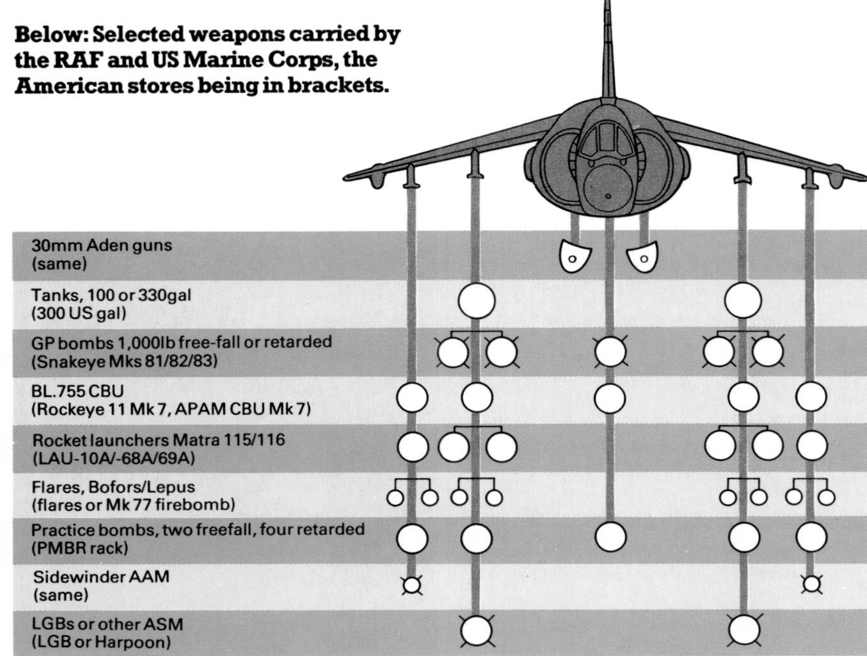

Harrier in Service

Since April 1969 Harriers have flown half a million operational hours, almost all under conditions of peculiar severity. Unlike other aircraft, a proportion of this time has been high-power hovering balanced on four thunderous jets which often kick up debris from the ground. Yet FOD (foreign-object damage) has been less than for many conventional aircraft, and even the birdstrike problem has been no worse than for other low-level attack aircraft. Unexpectedly, the Harrier has also turned out to have unique advantages in air combat; surely all fighters will one day have vectored thrust?

XV276, the first of the six DB prototypes, made its first hover on 31 August 1966. Subsequent development was most successful, and progressed from a simple unpainted aircraft with a long nose probe, no guns or pylons, six blow-in inlet doors and four vortex generators on each wing, to aircraft indistinguishable except to a real expert from the first production Harrier GR.1 (GR, ground attack and reconnaissance). The latter aircraft, XV738, was the first of 60 ordered in early 1967, sufficient to equip an OCU (Operational Conversion Unit), a front-line squadron in Britain and another in RAF Germany.

In the course of 1967 numerous carry-trials flights at Dunsfold proved various external stores, and the process gained momentum in 1968 with five aircraft at the Aeroplane & Armament Experimental Establishment, Boscombe Down. Indeed, it has never stopped, and even today new weapons and EW fits are being cleared both in Britain and in the USA. Among the early clearances was the AIM-9B Sidewinder AAM, envisaged as a light self-defence weapon. Photographs of the installation, on the outboard pylons, were taken in January 1968; but no provision was made for it in RAF Harriers, so in Operation Corporate 14 years later the trials had to be flown as a crash programme!

In early 1968 Hawker Siddeley Aviation hosted the media at Dunsfold. Though it was a new experience to witness a pirouetting display by seven jump jets, many of the pressmen failed fully to appreciate that they were witnessing the start of a new era in warfare

Above: A brace of RAF Harrier GR.3s on a training mission in 1980 from 233 OCU, Wittering. Individual aircraft letters are in pale blue above the fin flash. Aircraft L, on the right, is probably XV807. Each aircraft is carrying two tanks and two practice-bomb carriers.

Right: When new this Harrier was designated as a Hawker Siddeley AV-8A, or Harrier Mk 50, and it is shown in its original markings in service with VMA-231. Note the big tactical VHF mast above the fuselage, the bolted-on probe and the light practice bombs carried in tandem.

Above: This US Marine Corps Harrier was the fourth to be built and the third to be delivered (on 12 March 1971), but it was photographed in July 1982 after updating to AV-8C standard. For most of its career it has served with VMA-513.

Above left: Four AV-8As of the US Marine Corps – probably from VMA-513, though this is not certain – en route to air/ground rocket firing during a practice deployment to MCAS Yuma, Arizona. Attacks would be made in 20° dives.

in which airpower can be provided with neither airfields nor aircraft carriers. Bob Lickley, assistant managing director, reported good results with dropped stores, dry contacts with Victor K.1A tankers, ceiling climbs to beyond 50,000ft (15·24km) and the company's offer to sell Harriers at "£750,000 to £1 million, depending on quantity and equipment". He also announced further growth in thrust of the Pegasus, all of which could be translated into greater fuel or weapon loads.

During 1968 a massive effort was made to perfect the nav/attack system, which in some respects was new to British experience and at the time was fully competitive with anything flying elsewhere. Even in 1967, when it worked properly, accuracy of the basic inertial system degraded at less than 1nm (1·15 miles, 1·85km) per hour, and weapon delivery accuracies were the best ever achieved with RAF attack aircraft, and similar to results with the contemporary F-111. By autumn 1968 the main advance had been reliability and consistent performance. Several important trials were also flown from ships, following earlier experiments with P.1127s, as related in the next chapter.

Enter a customer

Overseas interest in the Harrier was in some places intense, though in most cases without the slightest thought of purchase. The only serious acquisition interests were shown by a few navies, and in any case Hawker Siddeley's main marketing effort was a low-key one aimed at educating military aviators whose usual understanding of vectored-thrust V/STOL was based on deeply rooted misconceptions. It was certainly a great surprise when, at the 1968 Farnborough air show, a commissionaire at the Hawker Siddeley chalet announced that at the door were three officers of the US Marine Corps who would like to fly a Harrier!

In fact, the Marines had been looking at the Harrier for eight months. One of the Corps' basic needs is effective airpower over a beach-head where its tough "Leathernecks" might be making an assault on a foreign shore. It had the choice between helicopters and total reliance on the giant carriers of the US Navy. The best helicopter seemed to be the Lockheed AH-56A Cheyenne, incredibly complex and costly and yet seemingly vulnerable because of its modest speed. For eight years a further alternative had been sought in SATS (short airfield for tactical support), but this meant the beach assault had to arrive complete with shiploads of aluminium planking, gas-turbine catapults, arrester installations and much more, as well as a complete Seabee construction battalion to fasten it all together. There had to be a better answer.

From the 1950s, largely because of the unswerving belief of Col, later Gen, Keith B. McCutcheon, the Corps had decided that the future lay with a V/STOL, when the technology matured. Though the Marines had played no part in the TES, they had carefully studied the six XV-6A (Kestrel) aircraft which from 1966 flew from Edwards, NASA-Dryden, NASA-Langley and the Naval Air Test Center at Patuxent (Pax) River, where Marine pilots at last flew them. In April 1966 an XV-6A flew from the LPD (assault ship) USS *Raleigh*, and for the first time the Marines began to wonder if the little Hawker jet might not represent the germ of something they could use. There was no doubt it had all the performance they wanted, and it had the most flexible basing possibilities anyone could wish. But not until 1968 was it clear that the more powerful version, the Harrier, might be able to do a useful job in the close-support mission.

Thus, despite the outpourings of the uninformed media, whose universal view in the United States was "the Harrier couldn't carry a box of matches across a football field", Gen Leonard C. Chapman, Commandant of the Corps, ordered that the British aircraft should be thoroughly evaluated. Brig-Gen Johnson came to England with two outstanding pilots, Col (later Gen) Tom Miller and Lt-Col Bud Baker. The Minister of Technology granted each Marine pilot ten flights, and their searching evaluation confirmed that the Harrier could do rather more than the popular American – and, in fact, world – opinion, and was close to being the ideal air weapon that the Corps had long dreamed of. It quickly drew up plans for a buy of 114 aircraft, sufficient to support four 20-aircraft squadrons plus training and attrition.

At Christmas 1968 the Marines announced their interest, and that they had received Department of Defense (DoD) approval for an initial buy of 12 aircraft to get the programme started. Funds for these were slashed from the DoD budget in the final rounds of Congressional cuts in January 1969, but this was only a temporary setback. A line

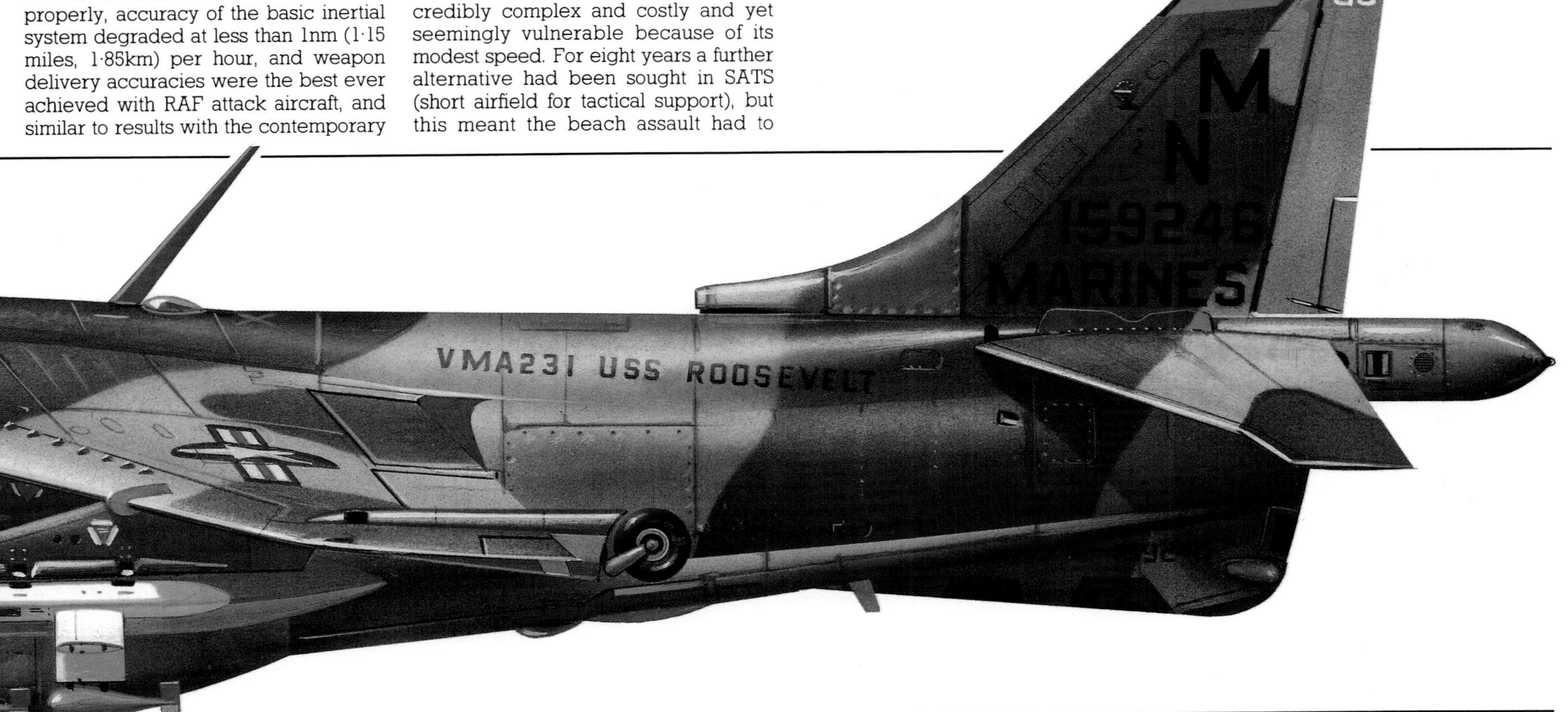

item in the FY70 (Fiscal Year ending 30 June 1970) budget was $58 million for 17 new F-4J Phantoms. The Marines willingly gave up these aircraft and used the money to pay for the initial 12 Harriers, which received the US designation AV-8A. They were to be made in Britain, and as nearly as possible copies of the RAF Harrier. Subsequent AV-8As were to be licence-built in the USA, and Baker and Miller visited all the chief American aircraft companies. Instant interest came from Douglas, which saw the AV-8A as the replacement for its own A-4 Skyhawk. But the California company had just come under the control of MCAIR (McDonnell Aircraft of St Louis). To everyone's surprise, not only did Sandy McDonnell express support, but he even got the British V/STOL project transferred to MCAIR! A 15-year agreement was signed with Hawker, not only for making the AV-8A but also for mutual exchange of all subsequent vectored-thrust V/STOL data and drawings. Pratt & Whitney signed with Rolls-Royce in October 1971 for joint future development of the Pegasus, under the US designation F402, with an option on a manufacturing licence.

In October 1969 the US Navy (on behalf of the Marines) and in January 1970 the USAF carried out evaluations of Harriers at Dunsfold. Both reports were highly positive, despite the tragic death on 27 January 1970 of Major Charles R. Rosberg, USAF, who got into uncontrollable roll during the tricky narrow band of airspeeds accelerating away from a VTO, when a flat turn or yaw is dangerous. This was the first fatal accident to any Hawker jump jet.

One of the changes specified in the AV-8A was the new Pegasus 11, with increased mass flow, improved water injection and turbine cooling and further revisions to the fuel control. This went into production as the Mk 103 for the RAF and Mk 803 for the AV-8A, but in fact these engines were too late for the first ten AV-8As which were delivered with Mk 802 (Pegasus 10) engines. Another obvious change was clearance with American ordnance, and the USMC interest in air combat prompted the obvious carriage of AIM-9 Sidewinder missiles. Though these had been fitted to a P.1127(RAF) at the A&AEE, the wiring was never installed. Amazingly, after the wiring to fire Sidewinders had been designed and fitted for the AV-8A, the RAF insisted that it should be specially *omitted* from its own Harriers, thereby causing a "crash" modification programme in April 1982! The Marines planned to replace the Aden guns at an early date, but these soon built up such a fine reputation they have remained in use to this day, even though they do not fire standard US ammunition. American communications radio, IFF and certain other avionic items replaced British equipment, an armament safety switch isolating the weapon circuits whenever the main landing gear oleo was compressed was fitted, and a direct manual throttle for use in emergency was also specified.

Below: Rising above the solid century-old ironwork of St Pancras station, London, XV744 was a very new GR.1 when it took part in the transatlantic race to New York City in May 1969. It had 100gal tanks, probe and bolt-on ferry wingtips.

While the AV-8A programme got under way, deliveries began of Harrier GR.1s to the RAF. The first aircraft, XV738, had flown on 28 December 1967. Carriage and weapon-release trials and nav/attack refinements occupied 1968, and in January 1969 the first RAF unit, the Harrier Conversion Unit, was formed at Dunsfold. The first delivery to an operational squadron, appropriately No 1 Sqn, based at Wittering, took place on 18 April 1969. On paper No 1 had actually received XV741 and 744 on 9 April, but both were diverted to take part in the transatlantic air race held in May. They were fitted with ferry tips, 100gal (455lit) tanks and refuelling probes and flew from the centre of London to the centre of New York and back. The first takeoff, from a disused coal-yard at St Pancras station, was notable for the amount of coal-dust blown over assembled dignitaries. The NY pad was a site at the Bristol Basin, in mid-Manhattan, so named because it had been filled with rubble from bombed buildings in Bristol, home of the Pegasus! Times for the 3,490 miles (5616km) were 5h 57min westbound, the best of any competitor, and 5h 31min eastbound.

Entry into service

QFIs (qualified flying instructors) who had completed Harrier conversion at Dunsfold then trained pilots of No 1 Sqn, followed in due course by Nos 4, 20 and 3 (in that order) forming a wing in RAF Germany at Wildenrath, the total RAF buy having been increased as listed in the Appendix. In early 1970 the HCU was restyled 233 OCU (Operational Conversion Unit) and moved to Wittering. It was true to RAF form that all the early Harrier conversion was done without the benefit of a dual two-seater, though this had been studied at Kingston since 1960. Some of the early two-seat P.1127 studies were novel, but reflected the unusual problems of putting a second cockpit in such a tight-knit V/STOL with four nozzles disposed around the CG. It was

Below: XZ146, an RAF two-seater, seen at Dunsfold in 1978 after it had been updated to T.4A standard with RWR and LRMTS. Curiously, it still has the original short fin. The same machine is seen above in its final paint scheme.

Below: Here XZ146 (see below) is shown resplendent in the markings of RAF No 4 Sqn, based at Gutersloh and carrying guns and bomb pods.

Below: In contrast, USMC 159380 is seen serving with VMA(T)-203 with the definitive tall fin, but of course no RWR, LRMTS or gun pods.

eventually clear that the only solution was a direct stretch of the fuselage with tandem seating.

When the RAF got round to drafting a requirement (ASR.386) for a two-seat Harrier, it made life harder by demanding that the aircraft should be able to take its place in the operational inventory, flown from the front seat with normal fuel and weapons. It was by no means certain that this was achievable, but once a contract for two two-seat development aircraft (XW174-5) had been received in 1967, work began in earnest. It was only rendered possible by the continued dramatic increases in thrust of the engine, because a two-seater was clearly going to be appreciably heavier.

Right: G-VTOL, the British Aerospace civil demonstrator, churning up the desert during a rolling vertical landing on an overseas trip in 1973. This aircraft has full "airways" avionics, and can go at short notice anywhere in the world.

It is simple to list the design changes in producing the two-seat Harrier T.2 (T = trainer), but in fact it was no simple task. The nose, with pupil cockpit, was cut off and moved 47in (1·19m) forward. The instructor cockpit was inserted in the gap, at a level some 18in (457mm) higher than the pupil. To provide room for the rear seat and pressure bulkhead, the cabin air-conditioning system was removed from its previous location immediately behind the seat. It was replaced by a new system, of greater capacity matched to the volume of the dual cockpits, packaged in the large new fairing behind the canopy. The latter was redesigned as a single large framed structure hinged open along the right side. To reduce the pitch moment the F.95 camera and inertial platform were moved from the nose to a location under the rear seat, immediately in front of the nose gear. To maintain control power, the forward RCV was brought even further into the nose, being moved forward by 56in (1·42m). To balance the destabilizing effect of the larger nose the entire tail was moved 33·3in (846mm) to the rear, and the vertical fin enlarged by mounting it on an extra root section 11in (279mm) high. The ventral fin was changed in shape and enlarged. The fuselage tailcone was lengthened, partly to increase the moment arm of the pitch/yaw RCVs and partly to house ballast to counter the extra mass ahead of the CG. This ballast, and the instructor seat, are removed when the aircraft is flown as a single-seat combat aircraft. The horizontal tail was not altered, apart from adding shot-filled tubes near the tips to damp resonance caused by the fact that the long fuselage has a natural frequency that is a sub-harmonic of that of the tailplane. Thus, ground crew must be careful never to bolt a single-seat tailplane on a two-seater.

The first two-seater flew on 24 April 1969, but this crashed from fuel-control contamination and the real development was done with XW175. There were few problems apart from inadequate yaw (weathercock) stability at high AOA (angle of attack). This proved a most intractable problem, taking until the late summer of 1971 to cure. By this time pro-

1 Classical dispersed operation

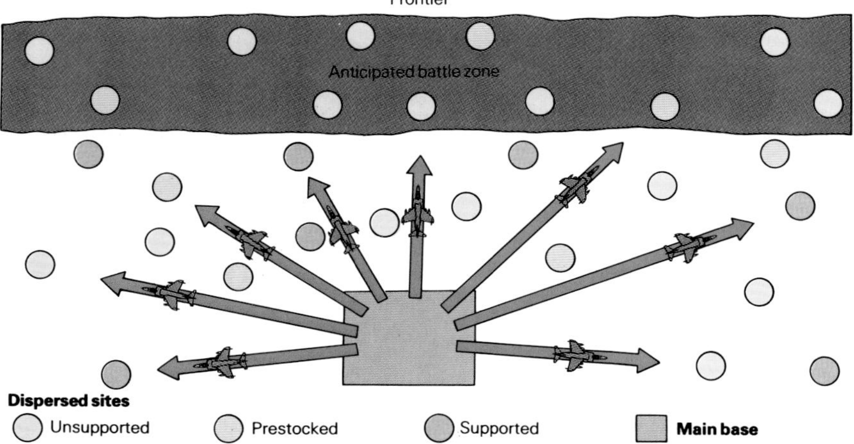

2 Operations from unsupported sites

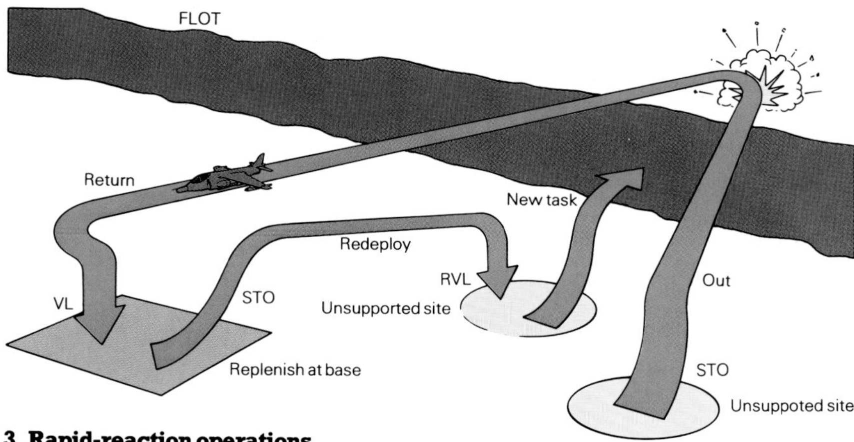

3 Rapid-reaction operations

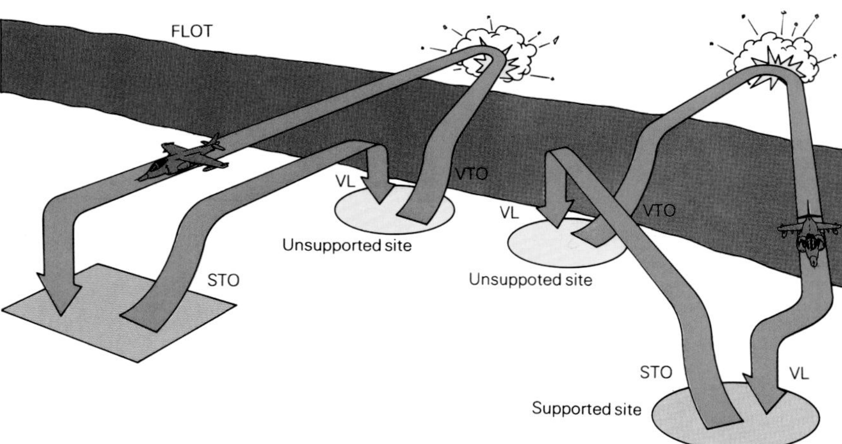

4 Operations from prestocked sites

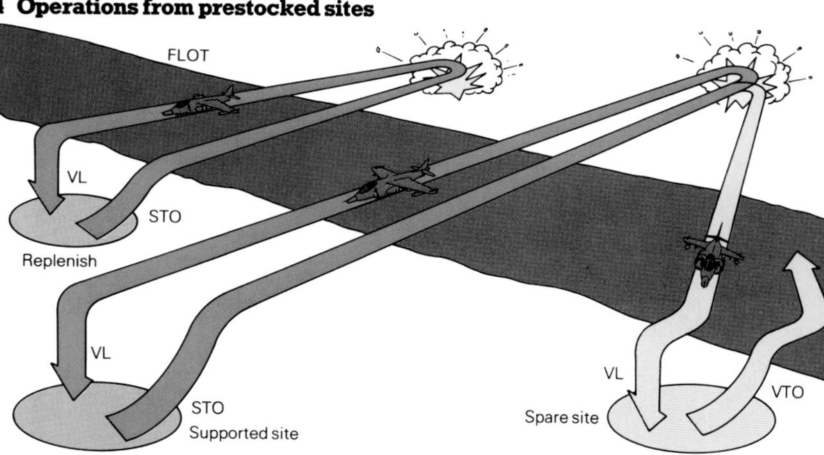

1 In the classical pattern Harriers work from a main base near the land battle but disperse away from it in emergency or whenever the need arises. This stylized plan view shows a front-line area dotted with the three kinds of dispersed site.

2 Here the main base has been heavily attacked and is being used only as a logistics centre. The unsupported sites are bare plots used as "ground loiter" positions close to the FLOT (forward line of own troops). Pilots are summoned by radio communications.

3 This is the "cab rank on the ground" concept, which among other things saves fuel compared with the cab rank method of 1944. Note that one dispersed site here is big enough for an STO, which gives more payload or mission endurance.

4 Here there is no main base, and all operations are from prestocked sites (with fuel, weapons and a few support personnel) or supported sites (which also have full frontline servicing and briefing facilities, and radio communications).

Above: Harrier GR.3s of RAF No 1(F) Sqn temporarily in removable Arctic camouflage while on detachment to RNorAF base Bardufoss in 1979. The occasion was a NATO exercise called, appropriately, Cold Winter.

duction T.2s were in service, and many were modified with the final cure, which, after several adjustments, is a broader vertical tail with 18in (457mm) extra height, together with automatic opening of the airbrake to 26° whenever the horizontal tail is commanded to large negative angles.

Prolonged further trials, including carriage of stores, were flown with the first production T.2, XW264, which first flew on 3 October 1969. Subsequent details of production mark numbers, serials and numbers built are given in the Appendix at the back of the book. The RAF uses the two-seaters for pilot conversion at 233 OCU and on each Harrier squadron for weapon-delivery instruction, instrument ratings and various other checks. From 1971 the two-seaters greatly eased conversion problems, improved general proficiency standards and enabled inexperienced first-tour pilots to join Harrier squadrons.

Units in operation

Operational flying was approached in easy stages. An early overseas deployment was No 1 Sqn's armament practice camp at RAF Akrotiri, Cyprus, in March 1970, when a great deal of live firing at ground targets was combined with a long transit flight, but without using air refuelling. Then followed a busy round of off-base operations in various climates, Tacevals (tactical evaluations) in which the operational performance of a unit is numerically assessed in simulated front-line conditions, introduction of a succession of aircraft improvements, and solution of some of the major operating problems, other than the intractable one of birdstrikes. At first "everything but the kitchen sink", and sometimes that too, was taken to each dispersed site in order to make things as much like a well-equipped airfield as possible. Though NATO has never attempted to emulate the Warsaw Pact air forces in spartan dispersed-site exercises, at least the RAF Harrier squadrons have acquired great experience in how to sustain high-intensity operations for a week or more without going near an airfield and with the minimum of special equipment. Even so, such an exercise still needs eight C-130 loads, not counting fuel.

No 20 Sqn converted from Harriers to Jaguars in 1977, and Nos 3 and 4 were brought up to 18 aircraft each and relocated at Gutersloh, nearer East Germany than any other NATO airfield. Both units have scored maximum possible marks in many exercises, including NBC (nuclear, biological, chemical) simulations. On most exercises each Harrier has flown an average of from four to 12 combat missions a day, with full briefings and complete changes of weapons and other "consumables", but without inertial realignment. In Exercise Oak Stroll in 1974 a total of 24 serviceable aircraft flew 1,121 missions in nine days, while in Big Tee (Tee = Tac eval exercise) in the same year No 1 Sqn flew 364 missions in three days with 12 aircraft, one machine flying 41 sorties. The CO said "Try *that* with an F-teen jet!"

The STO technique

Very soon it was obvious that the optimum type of mission is STVOL (short takeoff, vertical landing), the STO greatly increasing possible weapon loads for a given mission radius. The technique could hardly be simpler: the aircraft is lined up with the park brake on, the ASI bug (marker on the rim of the airspeed indicator) is set to a pre-computed takeoff speed, such as 140

knots, and the nozzle angle stop locked at 50°. The throttle is then moved to 55 per cent, brakes released and the throttle slammed to 100 per cent. A quick glance to check that full power has been obtained, and then, as the needle rotates past the bug, the nozzle lever is quickly whipped back to the stop. The Harrier leaps off the ground, gear is retracted and, as the aircraft climbs away on a mixture of engine thrust and wing lift, the nozzle lever is inched forwards, at the same time raising the flaps, until at about 180 ASI the aircraft is fully wingborne. At speeds up to 400 ASI, with nozzles aft, a Harrier out-accelerates everything else in the sky.

Above: Taken in 1971, this picture shows the lavishly equipped kind of hide with which RAF Harrier units played early in the aircraft's career. In a real war hides might be more spartan, and less visible.

Curiously, in view of its major extra capability of vectored-thrust V/STOL, the Harrier is in almost all respects simpler to fly than other tactical combat aircraft. As explained in a later chapter, it can operate when all other jets are grounded. It can also be operated from small pads, platforms and heaving ship decks by pilots who have never even seen a ship previously. (The very important ski-jump technique appears in the next chapter.) The one standard departure from the STOVL operating routine comes when operating from unprepared surfaces, in which case an RVL (rolling vertical landing) is made, touching down with as much forward speed as the available run allows – typically 40 ASI – to minimise FOD (foreign-object damage) and recirculation of jet gas.

Below: An early GR.1 on Ministry trials in 1971, hovering near a simulated blasted runway while laden with guns, tanks, rocket launchers and recon pod.

From the earliest days of the P.1127 great attention has been paid to the increased importance of reingestion and FOD in V/STOL aircraft. Flow patterns round a hovering Harrier in ground effect are complex, and strongly modified by the extremely high energy supersonic blasts from the RCVs, but the underlying pattern is that there are four slightly divergent pillars from the main engine nozzles which spread out on impact across the ground. Jet temperatures are roughly 100°C for the front nozzles and 600°C for the rear (the RCV jets are at around 300°C), but absence of smoke means that the only way to see the jets is by "heat haze" light refraction. Air

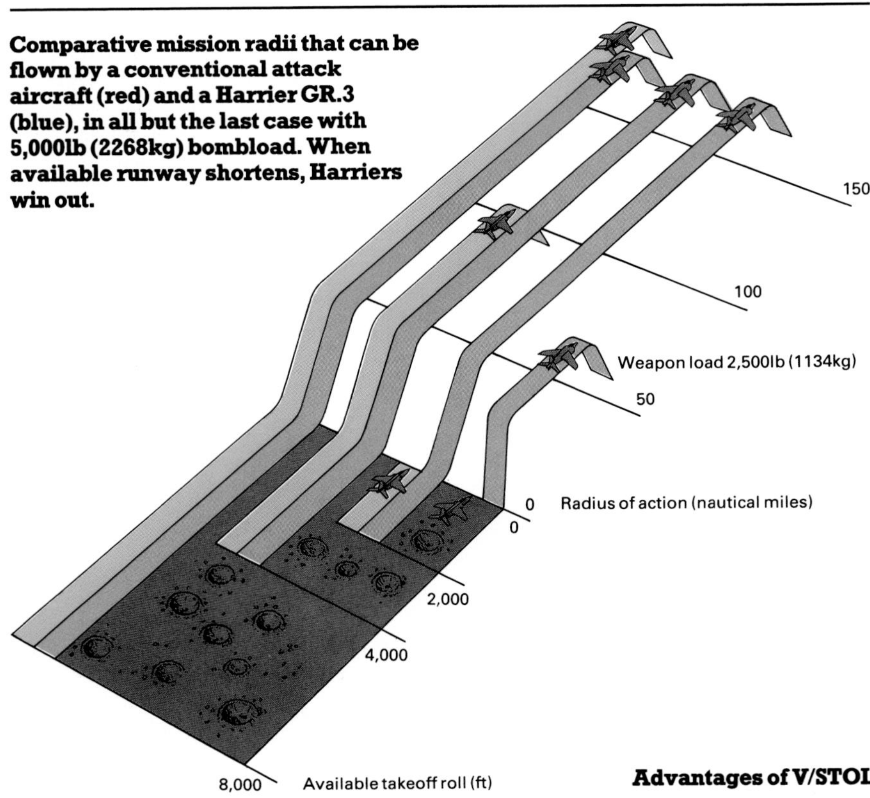

Comparative mission radii that can be flown by a conventional attack aircraft (red) and a Harrier GR.3 (blue), in all but the last case with 5,000lb (2268kg) bombload. When available runway shortens, Harriers win out.

Advantages of V/STOL

and gas spreads outwards along the ground, rapidly losing energy, but the flows spreading inwards, for example from the two left-hand nozzles, almost immediately meet the mirror-image flow from the other side of the aircraft. The only place to go is up, resulting in a fountain jet rising vertically and striking the belly of the aircraft. This might seem advantageous, like the fountain that supports the ball at a shooting gallery, but in fact the high-velocity flow round the fuselage tends to act like the air flowing over the curved surface of a wing and suck the Harrier downwards. It is the designer's task to arrange strakes and dams to contain this flow, rather like the design of an air-cushion vehicle, to create a high-pressure area that will more than overcome the suck-down and instead add to the lift.

RAF Harriers and related aircraft have a simple LID (lift-improvement device) in the form of the two gun pods. These break up the impacting flow and, even though it can freely escape past the landing gears to front and rear, create a region between the pods where pressure is significantly above atmospheric. When the pods are removed, their effect is achieved by fitting strakes along the belly in the same locations.

FOD is an enormous subject. One aspect is birdstrikes, which cause significant attrition of low-flying aircraft everywhere that there are birds. Peculiar to the Harrier is FOD caused by poor operating procedures, which at the least can leave the aircraft covered in dirt blasted from the ground, and at worst can write off the engine fan, or the complete engine, or the complete aircraft. Despite its large fan and sea-level airflow of 432lb (196kg)/s, the Pegasus is a tough engine, and the Hylite fan blades stand up particularly well to most FOD, but at the same time it is essential for all Harrier personnel, especially pilots, to bear the problem in mind.

This is especially important when operating from unprepared sites. The Harrier obviously needs to be as self-sufficient as possible, and though (surprisingly) ladders are still deemed essential for cockpit access, various changes have made the RAF aircraft normally independent of ground services. Electrical power has been considerably uprated, both by fitting the Mk 2 version of the Lucas APU, with electrical output raised from 1·5kVA to 6kVA, while the original pair of engine-driven 4kVA alternators have given way to the 12kVA machine which was fitted to the AV-8A from the start.

One reason for wanting more electrical power has been the introduction of

Above: Not many photographs are available showing Harriers making rocket attacks. One of them is this portrait of the very first production Harrier, after conversion to GR.3 standard, on a range in Sardinia.

additional equipment. Of course, the recon pod consumes a little power, and this is often carried by No 4 Sqn. All RAF Harriers in front-line service have since the late 1970s also carried two items that alter the appearance of the aircraft. One is the RWR and the other the LRMTS.

New equipment

The LRMTS (laser ranger and marked-target seeker) occupies the thimble extension on the nose. The Ferranti 106 laser, similar to that fitted to the Jaguar, is a Nd-YAG type which can be fired actively as a super-accurate measuring device which can be aimed by either the nav/attack system or the pilot within a 20° cone ahead. It provides target range, range-rate and angles, presented on the HUD. In the passive (MTS) mode it detects and locks on to any target illuminated with Nd-YAG (IR "black light") by friendly troops, providing the same weapon-guidance information as before. The ground illuminator and airborne receiver can be coded together to avoid spoofing IRCM (IR countermesures) or false lock-ons.

The RWR (radar warning receiver) is the MSDS ARI.18223, a typical 1960s-style installation which warns the pilot if his aircraft is being illuminated by a hostile radar. It covers the E to J frequency bands, of wavelengths from 15 down to 1·5cm, and receives at two aerials (antennae) mounted at the tail, that near the top of the fin leading edge covering the 180° facing ahead and that at the tip of the tailcone covering the 180° to the rear. The installation is rudimentary, the warning in the cockpit being merely a four-sector display which illuminates any 90° sector in which a hostile emitter is operating, and indicates its frequency band. Audible warning can also be given. In later aircraft the RWR is linked with an EW installation, but until May 1982 nothing had been provided to protect RAF Harriers. This subject is dealt with in the chapter on Operation Corporate, where EW protection was suddenly needed.

While these items were being retrofitted, more powerful engines became

Right: LRMTS with the lid off, a Ferranti picture showing the nose laser of a GR.3 and particularly laying bare the gimballed optical system of Cassegrain-telescope type.

British Aerospace Harrier GR.3

Below: The RAF Harrier GR.3 is here illustrated with a selection of its ordnance. The very advanced Wasp missile (shown with a tube launcher) will not now be selected for use by the RAF. In the Falklands, GR.3s were fitted with the Royal Navy rocket launcher, with 36 tubes of 2in calibre (see pages 38-9).

1 AIM-9B Sidewinder AAM (for the Falklands campaign the improved AIM-9L, now in production in Europe, was quickly made available, and a twin carrier was also cleared for use)
2 Hunting JP.233 dispenser (short type)
3 Lepus flare
4 Drop tank, 100gal (455lit); for the Falklands conflict a 190gal (864lit) pattern was quickly cleared for use
5 Wasp ASM launching pod (12 round)
6 Wasp ASM (unloaded); development of this weapon has recently been suspended
7 Practice-bomb dispenser with bombs installed
8 BAe reconnaissance pod with horizon-to-horizon optical cameras, forward oblique and various low-level cameras, plus BAe D type 401 IR linescan
9 Gun pod (one of two) containing 30mm Aden and ammunition
10 Ammunition, typically 120-130 rounds per gun, maximum being 150
11 Two Matra retarded bombs, 882lb (400kg)
12 ML twin carrier with two GP bombs, 1,000lb (454kg)
13 Rocket launch pod and rockets; one common type is Matra 155 with 18 tubes of 2·68in (68mm) for SNEB rockets
14 GBU-13/18 Paveway II smart (laser-guided) bomb which was based on the British 1,000lb (454kg) free-fall bomb
15 Hunting BL.755 cluster bomb, 611lb (277kg), (contains 147 bomblets in seven bays)

Right: Almost all RAF Harrier flying in Europe has been from airfields. Here XV738, the very first RAF Harrier (also illustrated opposite) is making a rolling takeoff with 3 Sqn.

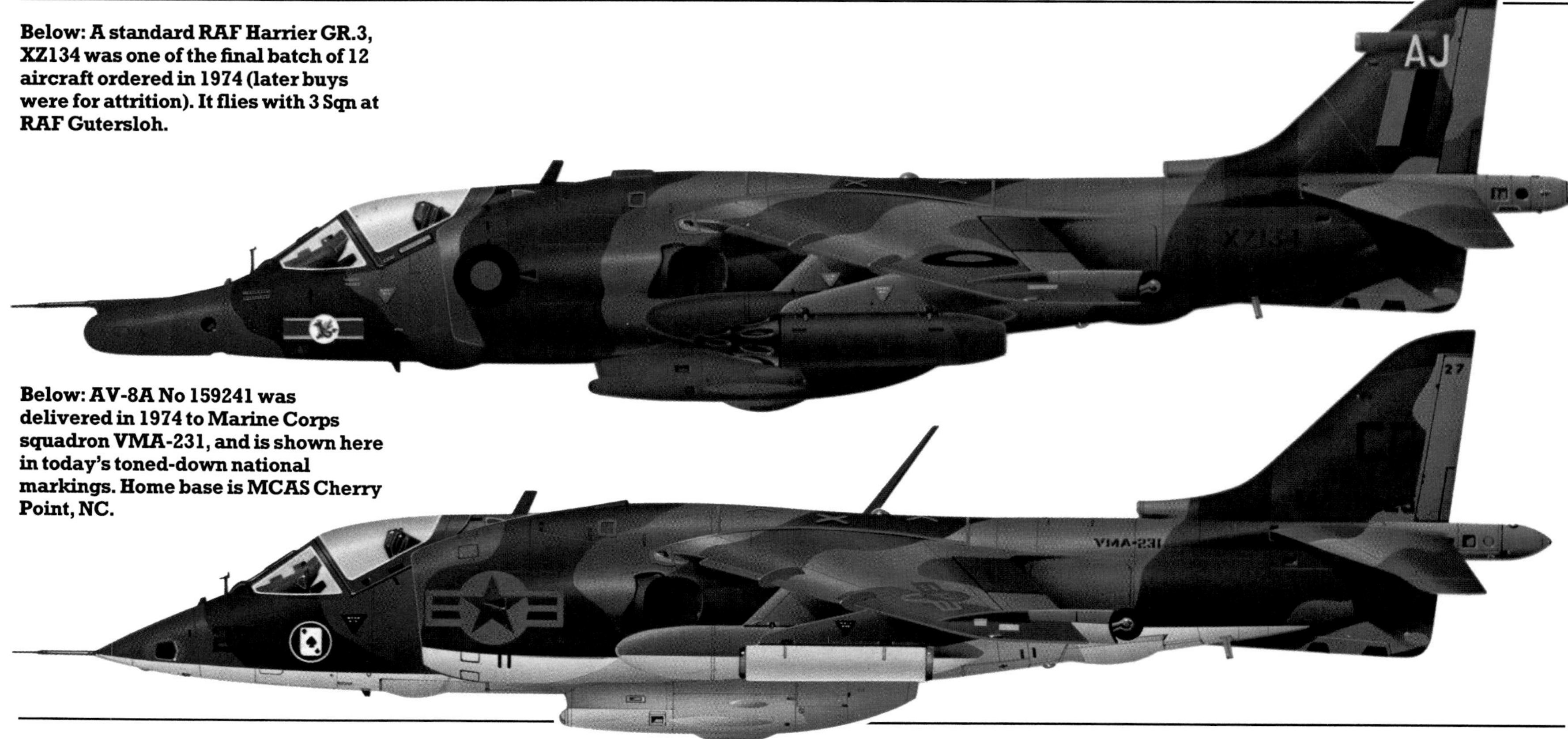

Below: A standard RAF Harrier GR.3, XZ134 was one of the final batch of 12 aircraft ordered in 1974 (later buys were for attrition). It flies with 3 Sqn at RAF Gutersloh.

Below: AV-8A No 159241 was delivered in 1974 to Marine Corps squadron VMA-231, and is shown here in today's toned-down national markings. Home base is MCAS Cherry Point, NC.

available. The Pegasus 102, production mark of the Pegasus 10 which had run in 1969 at 20,500lb (9299kg), introduced a higher turbine entry temperature and was a field modification. The uprated aircraft became the GR.1A and T.2A. The Pegasus 103 (Pegasus 11), rated at 21,500lb (9752kg), became available in 1972, and by 1976 had replaced all earlier engines. The mark numbers were changed to GR.3 and T.4, while new two-seaters fitted with the Mk 103 from the start were styled T.4A.

Clearly one of the shortcomings of first-generation Harriers, especially those of the RAF, has been a lack of any EW (electronic warfare) capability. The addition of a rudimentary RWR gives 360° coverage of hostile emitters, but what does the pilot do about it, except perhaps perform a smart change of course or start jinking? In the Falklands war we saw the embarrassing spectacle of chaff bundles being jammed in under the airbrake and between bombs and their ejector-release units! Now at last even the existing GR.3s are to get a proper EW kit, and as MSDS (Marconi Space & Defence Systems) estimates the potential order (with RDT&E and all spares) as worth "£100 million plus", each installation must be costed at more than the original price of the Harrier GR.1! MSDS is providing a new RWR which will be linked with an internal multimode RF jammer produced by Northrop. Known as Zeus, the system will be installed by BAe in RAF Harriers, perhaps from 1985, and MSDS/Northrop will market it elsewhere. It has not been announced whether Zeus will be specified from the start for the GR.5 described later, which will carry the outstanding BAe Dynamics Alarm anti-emitter missile.

As noted earlier, the USMC specified the Pegasus Mk 803 (export 103, also called F402-RR-401) but had to accept temporary installation of the Mk 802 (export 102, or F402-RR-400) in the first ten AV-8As. Deliveries began on 26 January 1971, and in late 1972 all AV-8As were cycled through NAS Cherry Point to bring them up to definitive standard. This included not only the Dash-401 engine but also the back-up manual fuel control, which was later added to RAF engines, for control following a bird-strike and consequent surge and flame-out. The planned American licence production never materialized because of the funding in small annual batches, in the teeth of opposition by Congress, which made transfer of production prohibitively costly. Thus, to the 12 FY70-funded aircraft were added 18 funded in FY71, 30 in FY72 and 30 in FY73. This left 24 for FY74, but in fact plans changed.

At the start the Marines suffered encouragingly low attrition, but after three years the rate increased sharply. Almost all incidents appeared to reflect on the pilot rather than the aircraft, and after prolonged enquiries it was decided that the AV-8A was a mount for ex-fighter pilots, who in the initial stages had been selected exclusively, rather than ex-helicopter pilots, who were finding it very hard to stay mentally abreast of what was happening. While the pilot selection procedures were tightened and training patterns revised, the decision was taken to buy some two-seaters in the final batch. Fearful of Congress withholding funds, the Marines

Below: RAF No 4 Sqn is the only unit which routinely carries out reconnaissance missions, using the multisensor pod on the centreline. These GR.3s were on a mission from Wildenrath in May 1983. Aircraft letters come yellow, orange or red.

Left: Marine Corps No 158385, the second AV-8A to be built, was delivered to VMA-513 on 5 February 1971 and is seen here on the deck-edge elevator of USS *Guam* during the AV-8A's first sea deployment.

stuck 100 per cent to single-seaters in the first four increments, and only felt safe in buying trainers in the final year. Extra costs of the two-seaters and various weapon clearances ate into the budget so that in the final year, instead of 24, only 20 aircraft could be afforded. These comprised 12 AV-8As and eight two-seaters, which were expected to be called AV-8Bs but instead received the designation TAV-8A.

Marine modifications

Modifications kept being made to the Marine aircraft, as a result of operating experience. Though the value of the INS was not in doubt, the Marines wanted a rough-and-ready nav/attack system needing no warm-up/alignment time and less skilled maintenance, and in 1973 the FE.541 system was replaced by a Baseline nav/attack system comprising the HUD fed with data from a Smiths IWAC (interface/weapon-aiming computer) which usually provides CCIP (continuously computed impact point) steering markers for air/ground visual delivery. Another change was to replace the Mk 9D seat by the American Stencel SIII-S3, on national policy grounds, and another was to fit a non-toppling attitude/heading reference system. Hawker had also fitted tactical VHF radio to many AV-8As, and to all two-seaters, with a large inclined aerial mast above the fuselage. The two-seaters are specially equipped with both tactical VHF and UHF, for use in the Airborne Tac Air Commander role in control of ground forces.

The first combat unit, formed in April 1971, was VMA-513 at Beaufort (pronounced Bewf't) MCAS in South Carolina, under Bud Baker. This squadron did many of the weapon trials at China Lake and Point Mugu, both in California. Next came the remaining units of Marine Air Group 32, all at MCAS Cherry Point, North Carolina: VMA-542, VMA-231 and training squadron VMA(T)-203. All have operated intensively from every kind of site or ship, including carriers (CV-42 *Franklin D. Roosevelt*), assault ships or Landing Platform, Helicopter (LPH-3 *Guam* in particular) and LHAs (Landing Helicopter Assault). It is largely because of Marines experience that Harriers made more than 13,000 missions from ships at sea before there was an accident of any kind, as noted in the next chapter.

In early 1970 Col Baker asked a fellow Marine, Capt Harry Blot, to be project officer for developing ACM (air-combat manoeuvring) with the AV-8A. Blot quickly decided the basic aircraft had excellent handling, a good engine that kept going in all combat situations, and an excellent thrust/weight ratio, but was penalized by its high wing-loading and poor rear view. Blot was under the impression that Viffing (VIFF, vectoring in forward flight) was common practice in RAF squadrons. In fact, Hugh Merewether had briefly toyed with "cracking the nozzles" at various speeds in the first 1127(RAF), and so had at least two RAF test pilots, but it was strictly absent from RAF Pilots Notes. Oddly, there had never been a deliberate attempt to see how well the Harrier

Left: Activity aboard USS *Guam* in 1974 as AV-8As of VMA-542 fly training missions. Each AV-8A is clean, without even guns, but inflight-refuelling probes are installed, for A-4 "buddy" contacts.

Defensive Break by Harrier

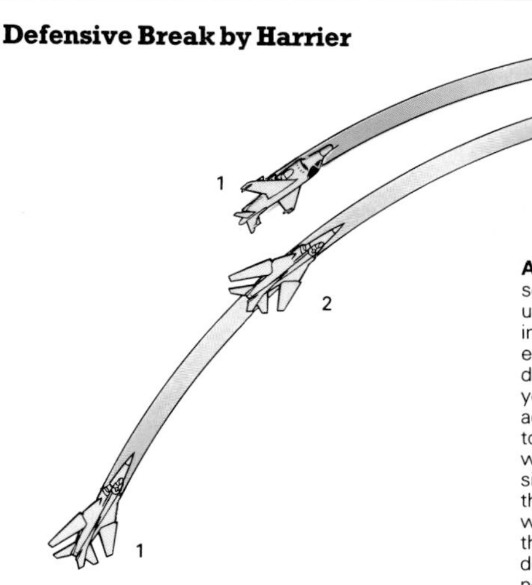

Above: The simplest of all Viff scenarios is when engine thrust is used to reduce turn radius or increase normal acceleration. In this engagement the Harrier RWR detects the enemy astern, but not yet in firing range (1). The Harrier accelerates, while pulling enough g to prevent the enemy from getting within firing parameters. This is the situation from (2) until at position (3) the faster enemy has just come within firing range. At the latter point the Harrier pilot performs his unique defensive break, pulling maximum normal acceleration and adding Viff. There is no way the enemy can avoid overshooting, and he then becomes an easy close-range target (4). Variables are numerous, one being that at (3) the Harrier pilot could even set the nozzles to 98·5° for more violent deceleration; another is that at (4) the half-roll may not be necessary, especially if AAMs are used.

Right: In these three sets of artwork the Harrier appears as an RAF GR.3, but in fact the drawings are based on originals stemming from the US Marine Corps, who pioneered the use of Viffing as an extra advantage in combat.

could look after itself if intercepted, but this is just what Blot was asked to do with the AV-8A.

Test sorties at the US NATC (Naval Air Test Center) were at a premium, so he decided to go straight to the limit: achieve 500-kt speed and then slam the nozzles to 98°! In his own words: "The airplane started decelerating at an alarming rate, the magnitude of which I could not determine because my nose was pressed up against the gunsight . . . the violence of the maneuver had dislodged me from the seat, and I was now straddling the stick, with my right hand extended backwards between my legs trying to hold on for dear life . . ." This was the start of the discovery that the Harrier can be a most difficult opponent in close combat.

The point has already been made that the Harrier is very small, smokeless and an odd shape, so that it is peculiarly difficult for an enemy to see at a glance what it is doing. Its IR signature is low and diffuse. On top of these factors, its ability to Viff was obviously worth exploring. NASA ran fresh trials with an XV-6A, while Blot organized computer simulations which showed, discouragingly, that Viffing would entail such loss in energy as to nullify any gains in manoeuvre. The computer program was then loaded into the twin-dome ACM simulator at MCAIR in St Louis, and this showed a very different picture. Most of it was impressive, but at low speeds there were results that conflicted with Blot's findings. He was, in particular, told that no aircraft could turn in the way he reported, while harsh demands at low speeds resulted in end-over-end tumbling resulting in a crash. Blot went back to NATC and spent many sorties carefully approaching these computer situations. He found that the uncontrolled tumbling was an error in the simulation, while the turn-rate discrepancy resulted from the actual aircraft being able to achieve a form of blown-wing effect, due to the pumping action of the jets, which with skill could result in turns that no other aircraft can equal.

Tests were also run in Britain, notably at the RAE, but the RAF has shown only marginal interest in ACM and its Harriers try to avoid combat, which is not part of their mission. The US Marine Corps, however, not only found exciting possibilities but even succeeded in getting British Aerospace (as Hawker Siddeley became on 1 January 1978) and Rolls-Royce to remove two limitations on Viff potential. The nozzles were modified with greater strength and a higher-

Climb and Flip by Harrier

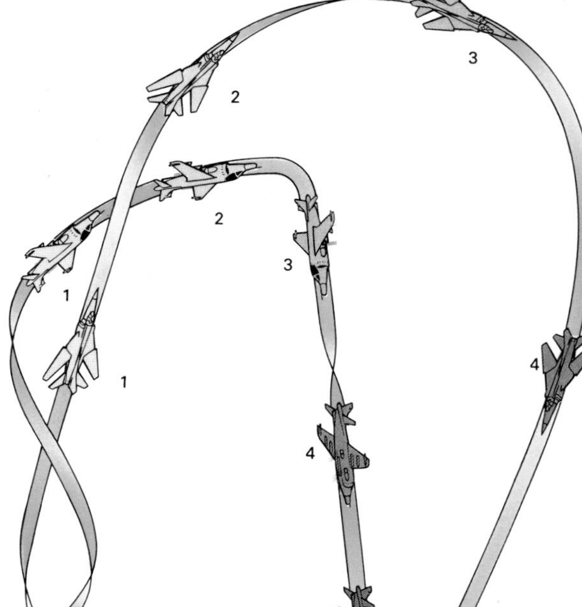

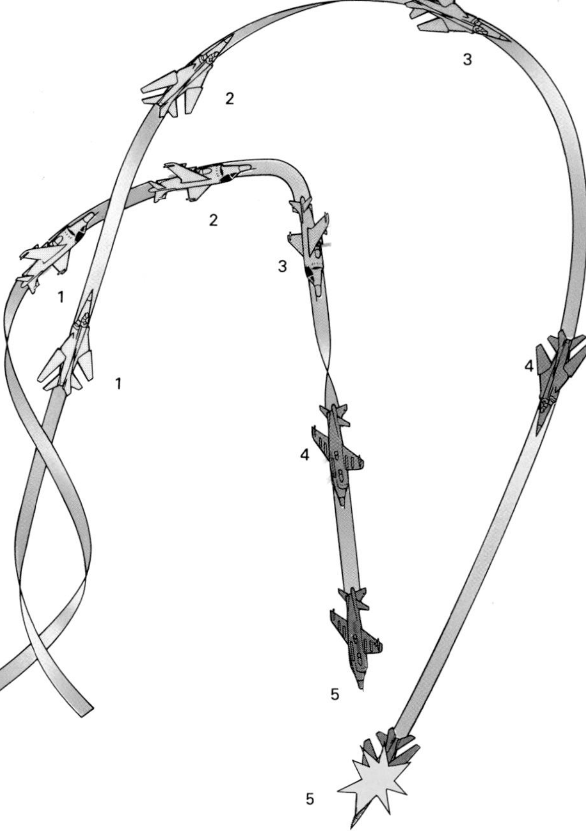

Right: In this so-called "climb and flip" the Harrier performs one of its numerous "impossible" manoeuvres, which are now part of the routine air-combat repertoire of all experienced US Marine Corps Harrier pilots. The sequence begins with the Harrier (whose trajectory is indicated by a blue line in all these illustrations) and its adversary (red line) climbing in a steep spiral and losing speed, the enemy close behind and eager to get within firing parameters before the Harrier can pull one of its tricks. From this position (1), with the enemy in close trail, the Harrier pilot using light stick forces pulls well past the vertical (2) and, as the speed bleeds away through the 200-knot level, he adds a small nozzle angle (3). The Harrier very quickly flips to a 90° nose-low attitude. The enemy has no option but to follow a semi-ballistic arching curve to end up going steeply downhill. Still travelling quite slowly, the Harrier goes into full reverse (4). There is no way the enemy can avoid going on down past what seems to be a Harrier stopped in mid-air. When the enemy gets to position (5) he presents the simplest possible target, for guns or AAMs.

Harrier as the Attacker

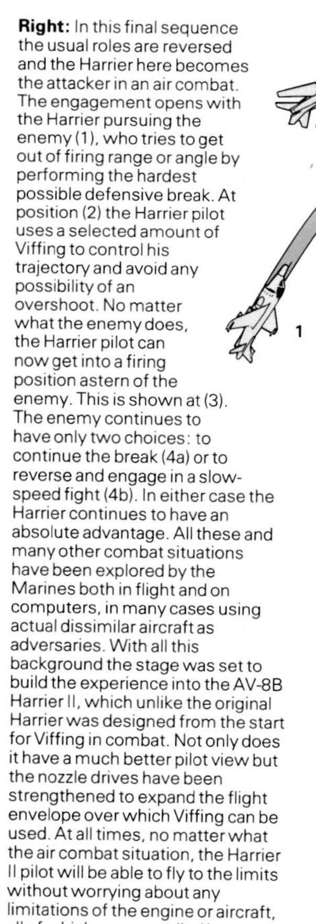

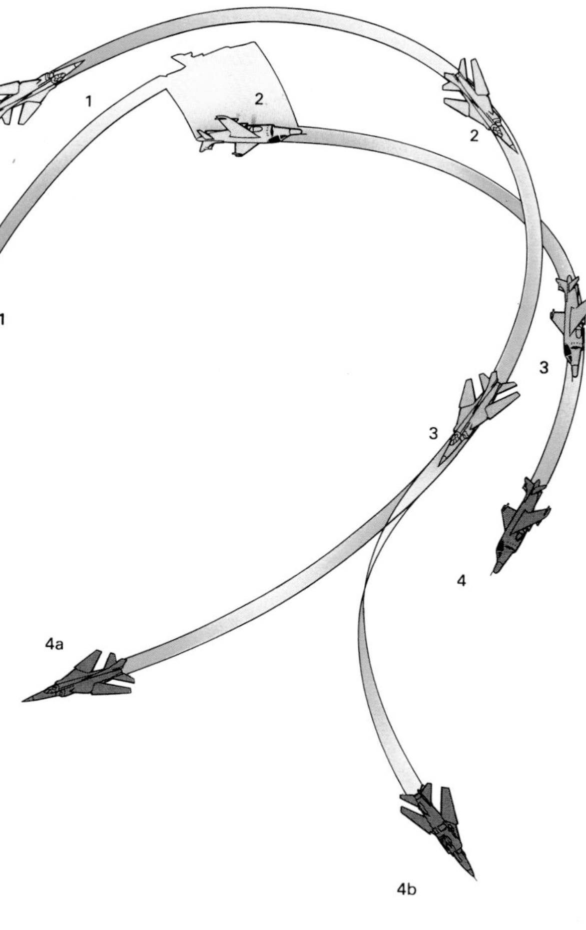

Right: In this final sequence the usual roles are reversed and the Harrier here becomes the attacker in an air combat. The engagement opens with the Harrier pursuing the enemy (1), who tries to get out of firing range or angle by performing the hardest possible defensive break. At position (2) the Harrier pilot uses a selected amount of Viffing to control his trajectory and avoid any possibility of an overshoot. No matter what the enemy does, the Harrier pilot can now get into a firing position astern of the enemy. This is shown at (3). The enemy continues to have only two choices: to continue the break (4a) or to reverse and engage in a slow-speed fight (4b). In either case the Harrier continues to have an absolute advantage. All these and many other combat situations have been explored by the Marines both in flight and on computers, in many cases using actual dissimilar aircraft as adversaries. With all this background the stage was set to build the experience into the AV-8B Harrier II, which unlike the original Harrier was designed from the start for Viffing in combat. Not only does it have a much better pilot view but the nozzle drives have been strengthened to expand the flight envelope over which Viffing can be used. At all times, no matter what the air combat situation, the Harrier II pilot will be able to fly to the limits without worrying about any limitations of the engine or aircraft, all of which are controlled by computers.

Left: Another photograph of Marine Corps rocket training on the Yuma ranges, in this case with monster Zuni rockets, which are the largest of their kind used by any Western air forces. The AV-8A, 158957 of VMA-542, was lost in 1976.

power drive, while the engine was provided with a combat plug, a screw-in turbine temperature control fuse, that for 2½ minutes allows the engine to give full power in wingborne flight, instead of a maximum of 75 per cent. This removed all restrictions on Viffing, at all speeds, attitudes and altitudes, without ever having to keep an eye on instruments. The potential discovered is described by Blot, now a colonel, as "absolutely eye-watering". It has been utilized to the full in the AV-8B.

In the mid-1970s the US Marine Corps began working on a major CILOP (conversion in lieu of procurement) programme to update surviving AV-8As for continued use through the 1980s. The scheme was put into operation at Naval Air Rework Facility, Cherry Point in 1979. It was planned to rework 60 aircraft, but the figure was cut by budget pressures to only 47, and these have been upgraded to AV-8C standard. The chief task is an airframe audit and rework under a SLEP (service life extension programme) for a further 4,000 hours flying. The LIDs of the AV-8B Harrier II (described later) are installed to enhance payload/range. Surprisingly, no laser or other weapon delivery system is installed, but EW gear is vastly augmented. The ALR-45 radar warning receiver is installed, with aft-facing aerials in the tailcone and forward-facing on the wingtips. A Goodyear ALE-39 dispenser for chaff, flares or jammers is installed in the rear equipment bay. An Obogs (on-board oxygen generation system) similar to that described in the AV-8B chapter is installed, and new radios include a new UHF and the KY-58 secure voice transmission system. AV-8C conversions are supported by kits from BAe Kingston-Brough division and MCAIR St Louis.

The plane in Spain

There is another operator of regular Harriers: the Spanish naval aviation, or Arma Aérea de la Armada. The Franco government began discussions in 1972, and, following a demonstration by chief test pilot John Farley which showed that the wooden deck of the old carrier *Dédalo* would barely get warm, far less burst into flames, a requirement was announced for 24 V/STOLs and an initial order was placed for six single-seat Harrier Mk 55s and two two-seat Mk 58s. Because it was feared a possible British Labour administration would tear up the deal, the order was placed via Washington and MCAIR, the aircraft being shipped to St Louis for final assembly and delivery as AV-8S and TAV-8S machines with BuAer numbers. They were assigned to Escuadrilla 008, with Spanish designation VA-1 Matador and, for the trainer, VAE-1. In 1977 a repeat order was placed for five more single-seaters. They are broadly to AV-8A standard, but with a broad VHF blade aerial for communicating with helicopters at sea. Operations from *Dédalo* and shore base Rota, near Cadiz, have been most successful and the new carrier, *Principe de Asturias* will operate 12 Harrier IIs.

Left: A pair of VA-1 Matadors of the second batch, alias Harrier Mk 55 or AV-8S, seen at BAe Dunsfold in company with G-VTOL. Because of the change in the Spanish government, there was no objection to placing this order direct with BAe.

Sea Harrier

Harriers of all kinds have operated from more ships, of more diverse types, than any other aircraft in history. Certainly no other aircraft comes close to the Harrier in logging over 13,000 missions from ship decks before there was a single incident involving damage to an aircraft. This chapter describes the special multirole Harrier developed for operations at sea. It can be based on large carriers, small carriers with ski jumps, small carriers without ski jumps, surface warships with a flat pad 80ft by 50ft (24m×15m), and also on container ships which 48 hours previously had no military equipment on board, and ships fitted with a novel Skyhook.

Above: Royal Navy No 809 Sqn was assembled at short notice by Lt-Cdr (now Cdr) Tim Gedge, and here most of its beautifully painted aircraft are seen immediately before departure from Yeovilton.

It is curious that, while some air staffs still ignore the destruction of their airfields during – if not immediately prior to – any future war, naval staffs the world over have recognized that the Harrier opens up totally new possibilities for deploying air power anywhere that a ship, not necessarily a carrier, can go. Back in February 1963 the P.1127 ran a programme of demonstrations from the carrier HMS *Ark Royal*, test pilots Bedford and Merewether discovering that operations from a deck were, they said, "simpler than from an airfield."

It may be that, in pursuing an elusive commonality with the RAF in 1963-64, and seeking the Mach 2 V/STOL P.1154RN, the Royal Navy was biting off more than it could chew. There would probably have been major problems in operating these heavy and expensive machines, though it is doubtful if they would have cost more than their replacement, the Spey-Phantom, which needs a large ship with full catapult and arrester gear. But the abrupt decision of the 1966 Labour government to terminate British fixed-wing airpower at sea, and to cancel the new carrier (CVA-01) then in design, brought a totally new situation. It is difficult for a service to argue against Government cuts in defence. If Their Lordships had said "What would we do if Argentina invaded the Falklands?" the Defence Minister in 1966 would have replied, in effect, "We really cannot concern ourselves with such unlikely eventualities!" So the fixed-wing Fleet Air Arm wound down to a full stop, and, after a while, saddened and perturbed people all over Britain stuck labels in their cars saying FLY NAVY.

By the late 1960s P.1127s, Kestrels, XV-6As and Harriers had demonstrated the complete absence of hassle in operating from many warships, some with nothing but a small helicopter pad, in various sea states with winds gusting to 40kt and with the ship doing anything from full speed to being at anchor. Several major shipbuilding companies were studying "Harrier carriers", with displacements down to a mere 6,000 tons, and without the need for catapults and arrester gear. The British Admiralty, having been informed that there would be no more fixed-wing seagoing airpower, and that there would be no replacements for the ageing fleet carriers *Ark Royal* and *Eagle*, was clearly faced with a lunatic situation. The government view was that future maritime airpower would be provided by the land-based RAF, a service already over-extended and unable to operate except around the shores of Britain! The US Navy could not be relied upon to provide airpower for purely British actions around the world, and the only possible, and obvious, alternative was to deploy a specially developed maritime version of the Harrier from a new class of V/STOL ship. Special ships were clearly indicated, though the V/STOL aircraft could also operate from simple helicopter pads on existing warships. The Admiralty was kept continuously updated on Hawker Siddeley's Maritime Harrier studies, yet, if the official story is to be believed, the decision was taken in 1968 to deploy a new class of V/STOL carrier – known as a "through-deck cruiser"

Below: Taken in the post-Falkland period in late 1982, this photograph shows a Sea Harrier FRS.1 streaming fuel from the jettison pipes. It has Training Sidewinder missiles installed.

Below: One of the third batch of production Sea Harriers, this FRS.1 is depicted with a single victory symbol. It later destroyed a second Mirage in the South Atlantic war while serving with 809 Sqn.

Left: France has always eyed the Harrier, and especially the Sea Harrier, with extreme interest. Here an RAF GR.1 is seen aboard the *Jeanne d'Arc*, a most useful ship of over 12,000 tons displacement, in October 1973. Sea Harriers would fit this ship ideally, though there might be political obstacles to such a mating.

Above: In 1971 RAF No 1(F) Sqn took their Harrier GR.1s aboard HMS *Ark Royal*, trying to assist a stupid political scheme whereby, in the absence of such ships, the RAF would provide air cover for the Royal Navy! No 1 has enough to do in connection with warfare on land, but the trials on this ship were impressively simple.

Below: When delivered the Sea Harriers were factory-finished in Royal Navy dark grey and white, with squadron tail badge, in this case 800 Sqn.

Below: In the South Atlantic aircraft were repainted for reduced visibility, as noted in the next chapter. This former 899 Sqn machine served with 800 Sqn.

(TDC) to avoid any hint that it might be used for the forbidden fixed-wing aircraft – which was to be designed *for helicopters only*. This is so beyond belief that it could be discounted, were it not for the fact that the initial form of TDC ship was indeed not optimised for fixed-wing V/STOL operation!

Part of the trouble was that, like many air staff at that time (1968-72), the RN Air Warfare department totally overlooked the air defence capability of the Harrier because it had (an official quote) "too short an endurance" and did not fly at Mach 2. Indeed, when RAF No 1 Sqn received an unprecedented clearance to go aboard RN carriers and fly combat missions (which the squadron did in March 1970, without the slightest trouble), the author was advised by an RN spokesman that "Of course, this idea that the fleet might be defended by Harriers is laughable!" Despite this, Hawker was asked by MoD to modify No 1 Sqn Harriers for shipboard operation by adding tie-down shackles to the outrigger gears and add a relay to the nosewheel steering so that, whenever the anti-skid brakes were switched off, the nosewheel steering would be engaged, preventing the aircraft from pirouetting round on a rolling deck. The RAF had plenty of other tasks for 1 Sqn – which could well have been wiped out on the

first day of a war, anyway – and in any case looked askance at the whole idea of a Maritime Harrier. The "light blues" doubted the ability of such an aircraft to intercept supersonic "Backfires", judged its ship to be costly and vulnerable, and feared that resurrection of naval air-power would result in cutbacks in the RAF's own budget. Meanwhile, the "dark blues" were not only mentally locked-in to the concept of Big Ship air-power but still wanted highly supersonic speed and a backseat crew-member.

Thus in true British fashion, the environment was confused and unfavourable. Despite this a few farsighted and dogged individuals, mostly at Kingston, kept on studying the possibilities for what in 1971 was called the Maritime Support Harrier. Though the RN Ship Department at Bath was well into the design of the TDC ship, its form was still somewhat fluid and there was no official requirement for it to carry any aircraft except helicopters. As for the MS Harrier, this too was fluid, because Hawker and MCAIR were busy with a next-generation aircraft, the AV-16 family, powered by the more powerful Pegasus 15 and in some forms capable of supersonic speed on the level. It was partly because of this vision of increased performance that, in early 1971, the RN Air Warfare staff began to consider an MS Harrier seriously; but the whole situation was made academic by the fact that there was no money.

The "Through-Deck Cruiser"

From the start of the TDC ship design it had been policy that these ships would serve in an ASW (anti-submarine warfare) role, act in a command/control role for both naval and air forces, and "make a contribution to area air defence". When the author asked what the latter meant he was told that it was interpreted as meaning a requirement for the Sea Dart SAM, and as finally designed a twin launcher for this missile represented virtually the only armament of these large and costly vessels! But at some time in late 1971 the Admiralty not only made a case for a Maritime Harrier but got

Left: An unusual formation off the Devon coast in 1981 made up of Sea Harriers of 899 Sqn (lead aircraft, tail code VL for Yeovilton), 801 (nearest, code N for HMS *Invincible*) and 800 (tail code H for HMS *Hermes*).

Treasury permission for it, and this not only resulted in a rethink of the TDC ship but also enabled Hawker to authorize a firm design programme. Rather than being an AV-16, the Maritime Harrier was to be a minimum-change Harrier, and when the Naval Staff Target for its previously forbidden new jet was issued in August 1972 it was seen to be written round the Harrier GR.3 with the minimum of alterations.

At last there was a programme for a V/STOL and a ship to carry it. Vickers received the contract for the first ship in April 1973, with a planned commissioning date of 1980. The TDC designation was gradually replaced by others:

Left: Today HMS *Invincible* has close-in Phalanx guns (small white thimbles at bow and stern) as well as her Sea Dart launcher. On deck in late 1983 were two Sea Harriers and a Sea King HAS.5.

official documents since 1980 have called these ships Command Cruisers, ASW Cruisers, AS Cruisers and CAHs (for Carrier, Assault Helicopter). At Kingston, Hawker received the development study contract for what was called the Naval Harrier. As studies had been going on in depth for several years previously, and money (equated with time) was tight, the job should have been completed quickly. Sadly, funding was administered in trickles, and often dried up entirely, and the planned go-ahead was delayed until January 1973, when an order for 24 aircraft was arranged. This was then delayed until June, when a complete review of the UK's defence commitments put the whole programme back into the melting pot. At last Hawker were advised in December 1973 that the go-ahead had been agreed, and would be announced the following week. What actually happened was a "fuel crisis", soaring inflation and industrial unrest. In 1974 there were two General Elections, a series of Defence Cuts and a near-total loss of hope. Then on 15 May 1975, as chief test pilot Farley and chief designer (Harrier) Fozard were on short finals at Dunsfold in the company Dove, the tower advised them "The BBC has just announced they're ordering 24 Sea Harriers!"

Designation of the aircraft is Sea Harrier FRS.1, for fighter/reconnaissance/strike. This versatility has rarely been attempted in any one aircraft, and it was not so much making the best of a bad job as the result of prolonged tests to establish the missions that can be flown from a small deck. The three roles actually spelt out in the Naval Staff Target were: (F) a 400nm (741km) radius of action at altitude carrying guns and Sidewinders against any ship-based or long-range shore-based aircraft; (R) sea search of at least 27,000sq miles (70 000sq km) in one hour at low level; and (S) at least 250nm (463km) radius (depending on mission profile) carrying a wide range of anti-ship or ground-attack stores, with accurate delivery.

In fact, mission radius and load were already known to depend on the takeoff run available, as with any other fixed-wing machine, and in the early 1970s a further major variable came into the picture: the ski jump. Before describing this, it is worth noting that by 1972 the Hawker test pilots had deeply explored Harrier operations from ships and come up with basic operating rules. If mission load is not important, the fastest reaction time, typically 90s from initiation of engine start to wingborne flight, is achieved with a VTO, and this also burns the least fuel (a matter of a mere 100lb, 45kg, to wingborne flight, compared with over 1,000lb (454kg), for an F-14). VTO enables aircraft to be spotted only 30ft (10m) apart, gives least sensitivity to ship motion and hardly ever requires the captain to alter course or speed. STO, on the other hand, enables heavier loads to be carried for any given radius, and a 500ft (152m) run with 30kt (55km/h) WOD (wind over the deck) gives exactly double the mission load that can be lifted from VTO. It was found that the ideal deck markings were white "tram lines" just 7ft (2·13m) apart, and that the takeoff clearway need be no more than 38ft (11·6m) wide. Harriers can line-up nose to tail and takeoff at full power with nozzles pointing aft. As for landings, these were always VL, and not only simpler but safer than using conventional carrier aircraft which hit the wires at 120kt (222km/h) relative speed.

Below: The island of HMS *Hermes* shelters XZ450, the first Sea Harrier to fly, on board for operational trials in the Irish Sea in October and early November 1979.

Sortie performance

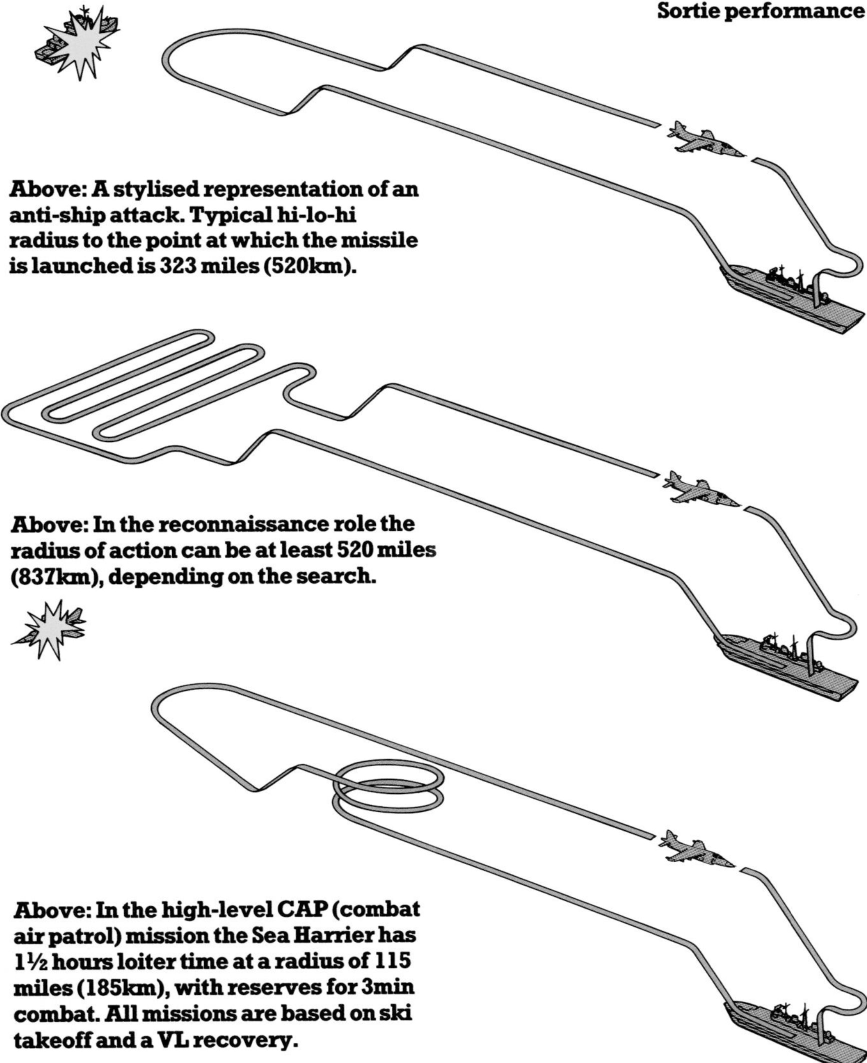

Above: A stylised representation of an anti-ship attack. Typical hi-lo-hi radius to the point at which the missile is launched is 323 miles (520km).

Above: In the reconnaissance role the radius of action can be at least 520 miles (837km), depending on the search.

Above: In the high-level CAP (combat air patrol) mission the Sea Harrier has 1½ hours loiter time at a radius of 115 miles (185km), with reserves for 3min combat. All missions are based on ski takeoff and a VL recovery.

Left: The DB (development batch) GR.1 Harrier XV281 made the first ski jump trials at the RAE Bedford, beginning with the ramp set at 6° on 5 August 1977. Here 281 goes off the end in the spring of 1978 with the ramp set at 15°, which is close to the best angle for operational use.

All this had been worked out in detail, and remains valid, and one particular series of trials was to take off at lower and lower airspeeds to investigate the limiting value of ASI and AOA, so that in any situation the maximum safe weapon load or minimum safe deck run could be assessed. Unlike a runway takeoff, the aircraft is instantly out of ground effect as it runs off the edge of the deck. On the other hand, it can be allowed to sink, because the deck is something like 50ft (15m) above the sea. But there is not a lot of time or space, and if total engine failure were to occur as the aircraft left the deck, it would go into the sea in 2½s, barely time for the pilot to eject. The dynamics of carrier flying have been studied by many people, some of whom in the mid-1940s were convinced landing gears could be replaced by flexible decks, while others believed it would help if the deck moved relative to the ship! Vectored thrust introduced a new situation, and an officer studying for an MPhil thesis at the University of Southampton came up with an answer whose importance is matched by its elegant simplicity.

Lt-Cdr Doug Taylor RN wrote his thesis on the subject of V/STOL operations from confined spaces – not necessarily ships – and showed that if the takeoff surface ends in an upward curve, great benefits ensue. As in any STO departure, there is a choice between length of run (for any given wind) and mission load. Taylor calculated that leaving with a trajectory inclined upwards at about 10° would add an upwards velocity component that would counter the "fall" resulting from insufficient airspeed, and thus compensate for an initially inadequate combination of jet thrust plus wing lift to balance the weight. In other words, the Harrier could start its flight with deficient lift (resulting from either too much mission load or insufficient STO run). Over the next ten seconds or so the thrust component from the nozzles set at 50° accelerates the aircraft to about 35kt (65km/h) higher airspeed, by which time there is no lift deficiency, and from this point on the aircraft can climb away normally. The big advantages are that it is possible either to take the air with a much heavier load or at greatly reduced airspeed, the entire initial trajectory is much higher above the sea or ground, and in the event of engine failure there is much more time in which to assess the situation and eject. In the case of a ship launch in severe weather, a ski ramp ensures a positive upwards trajectory even in the worst case of the ship pitching bows-down into the sea.

It is a yet further grave reflection on the British Official Establishment that from 1972 until mid-1975 there was very little support for the ski-jump idea, even though – at considerable expense – Hawker had done extensive studies and model tests which fully confirmed the most sanguine predictions. Indeed, the ruling view in the Admiralty was that such a disturbing idea was unwelcome, to the extent that Fozard called the ship experts "The Flat Deck Preservation Society". Doggedly, the first ship was built with a flat deck and a Sea Dart launcher bang in the bows on the centreline, so that a ski ramp would obstruct its arc of fire!

Ski-jump – at last!

In 1976 Hawker at last managed to get the MoD to fund the construction of a ski ramp for research on land, and this was built by Redpath Dorman Long at RAE Bedford. The first ski launch was made by P.1127(RAF) XV281 on 5 August 1977 at an exit angle of 6°. Subsequently this aircraft and others, including two-seaters, made 367 launches at angles up to 20°, at which angle the landing-gear oleos were just bottoming with the 4g vertical acceleration. Over 100 pilots had a go – they queued up – and Harriers took the air at 100kt (185km/h) below the normal STO speed of 142kt (263km/h)!

Not least of the many good features of this brilliant idea was that no aircraft modifications whatsoever were called for. This was doubly welcome, because the Sea Harriers had really become quite new aircraft, and in any case were,

British Aerospace Sea Harrier FRS.1 cutaway

1 Pitch RCV (reaction control valve)
2 Pitch feel and trim actuators
3 Inertial platform
4 IFF aerial
5 Yaw vane
6 Rudder pedals
7 Control column
8 Windscreen wiper
9 Instrument panel
10 Pilot's head-up-display (HUD)
11 Martin-Baker Mk 10H zero-zero ejection seat
12 Boundary-layer air exhaust ducts
13 Cockpit air-conditioning system
14 Engine oil tank
15 Alternator
16 Engine accessory gearbox
17 Auxiliary power unit (APU)
18 Starboard wing pylons
19 Starboard wing integral fuel tank
20 Aileron power unit
21 Starboard navigation light
22 Roll control RCV
23 Outrigger wheel fairing
24 Starboard aileron
25 Hydraulic reservoir
26 Plain flap
27 Anti-collision light
28 Water tank
29 Water filler cap
30 Flap hydraulic jack

Ski jumps save lives

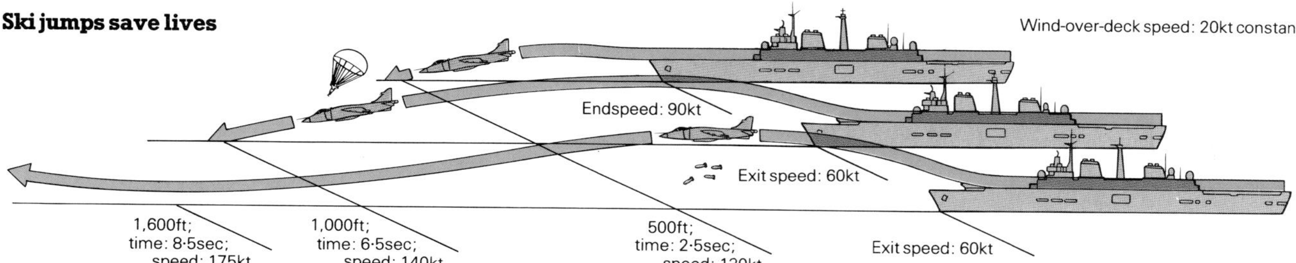

Above: Even though failure of the nozzle drive happens much less often than once in 10,000 launches, it is a factor to be reckoned with. In takeoff – jets aft – from a flat deck (top) the pilot has to eject, but has barely enough time to realize it before he hits the sea. With a ski jump at maximum weight he has almost three times as long (centre drawing). Alternatively, by smartly jettisoning external stores, he can even climb away despite the failure.

Ski jumps add weapons

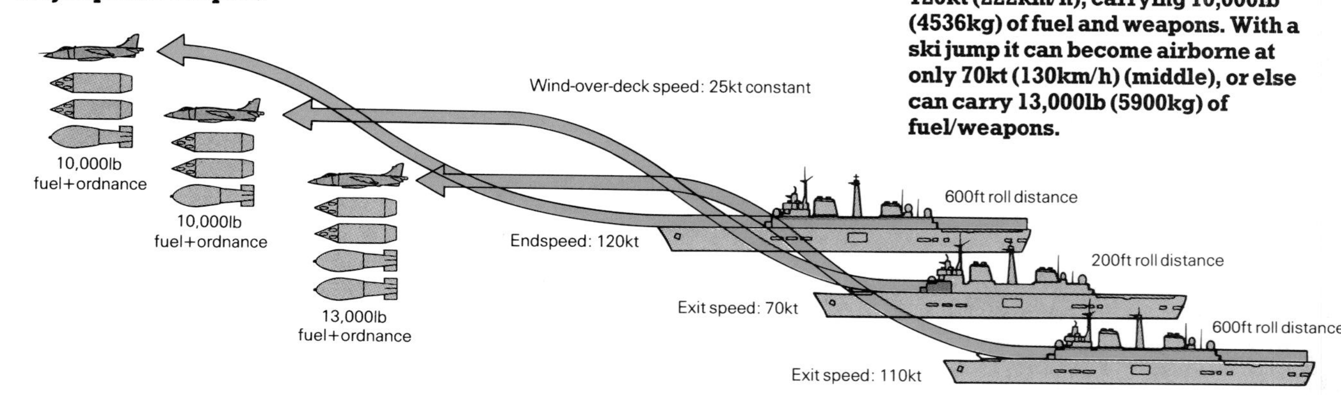

Below: Another, quite unrelated, benefit of the ski jump is that it enables a Sea Harrier either to carry a bigger load or to use a much smaller deck. In the traditional flat deck (upper ship drawing) the aircraft goes off the end after a run of 600ft (180m) at a speed of 120kt (222km/h), carrying 10,000lb (4536kg) of fuel and weapons. With a ski jump it can become airborne at only 70kt (130km/h) (middle), or else can carry 13,000lb (5900kg) of fuel/weapons.

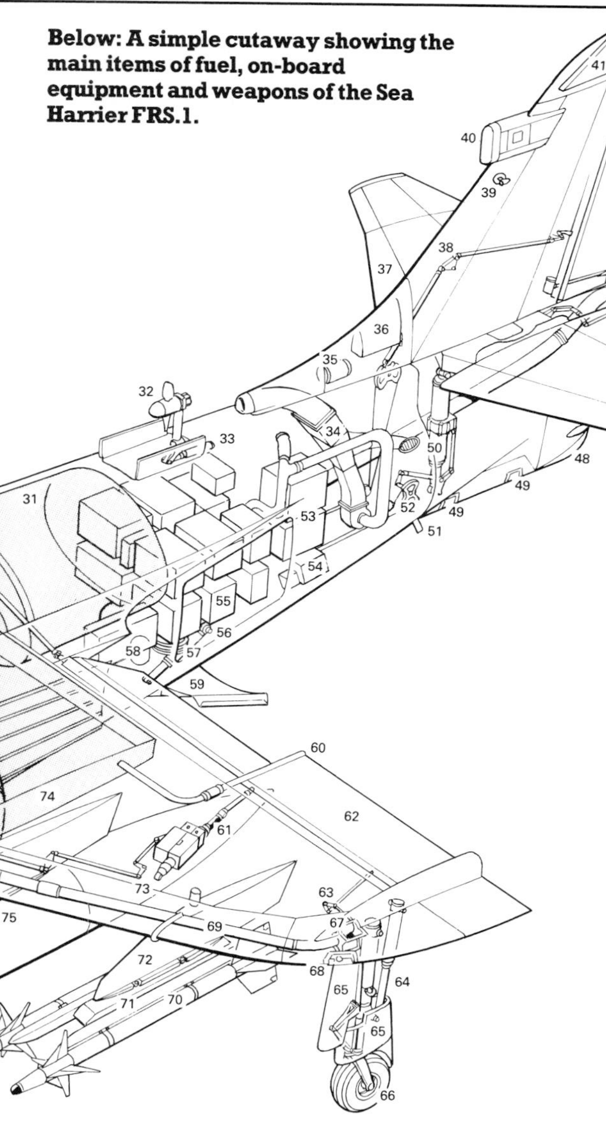

Below: A simple cutaway showing the main items of fuel, on-board equipment and weapons of the Sea Harrier FRS.1.

31 Rear fuselage fuel tank
32 Emergency ram-air turbine
33 Turbine release control
34 Equipment bay air-conditioning system
35 HF aerial tuner
36 HF notch aerial
37 Starboard all-moving tailplane
38 Rudder control linkage
39 Total-temperature probe
40 Forward radar warning receiver
41 VHF aerial
42 Rudder
43 Rudder trim tab
44 Yaw control RCV
45 Rear radar warning receiver
46 Pitch control RCV
47 Port all-moving tailplane
48 Tail bumper
49 Radar altimeter aerials
50 Tailplane power unit
51 UHF aerial
52 Control system linkages
53 Twin batteries
54 Chaff and flare dispensers
55 Avionics equipment racks
56 Airbrake hydraulic jack
57 Liquid-oxygen converter
58 Hydraulic-system nitrogen pressurising bottle
59 Airbrake
60 Fuel jettison
61 Aileron power unit
62 Port aileron
63 Aileron RCV mechanical linkage
64 Hydraulic retraction jack
65 Outrigger leg fairings
66 Port outrigger wheel
67 Roll control RCV
68 Port navigation light
69 Bleed air ducting
70 Twin AIM-9L Sidewinder air-to-air missiles
71 Missile launch rails
72 Outboard wing pylon
73 Aileron control linkage
74 Port wing integral fuel tank
75 190gal (864lit) drop tank
76 Rear (hot stream) swivelling exhaust nozzle
77 Inboard wing pylon
78 Mainwheels
79 Pressure refuelling connection
80 Ammunition tank
81 Main undercarriage hydraulic jack
82 30-mm Aden cannon
83 Fuselage flank fuel tank
84 Forward (fan air) swivelling exhaust nozzle
85 Engine monitoring and recording equipment
86 Ventral gun pod, port and starboard
87 Hydraulic-system ground connectors
88 Forward fuselage fuel tank
89 Rolls-Royce Pegasus Mk 104 vectoring-thrust turbofan
90 Supplementary air-intake doors, free floating
91 Nosewheel
92 Landing/taxiing lamp
93 Nosewheel hydraulic jack
94 Hydraulic accumulator
95 Boundary-layer bleed air duct
96 Pitot head
97 Radar hand controller
98 Ejection-seat rocket pack
99 Engine throttle and nozzle control levers
100 Doppler radar
101 Radar scanner
102 Radome, folded to port
103 Ferranti Blue Fox radar

Above: The family relationship imparted by Sir Sydney Camm is obvious as one of Yeovilton's Hunter T.8M Blue Fox radar trainers formates with a Sea Harrier of 899 Sqn. Every Sea Harrier pilot trains on the Yeovilton T.8Ms.

like the new ships, delayed by industrial unrest and other factors quite unconnected with the aircraft itself. The original build standard had been discussed in 1972, but it was not finalized until after the go-ahead in 1975.

Almost all the changes were confined to the front end, which was completely redesigned. Apart from this the main differences were: substitution of aluminium alloy for magnesium or Mg-Zr alloy to avoid sea-water corrosion (the only items not changed were the nose and outrigger wheels and the engine gearbox); a 4in (100mm) increase in fin height, mainly from building in the RWR as an extra section; addition of an emergency wheel-brake system; various system changes, including a liquid oxygen converter of a different make; addition of lashing lugs to the nose gear; increase in tailplane nose-up travel by 2°; increase in wingtip RCV roll power for use in turbulent ship wakes; and a switch to the Mk 104 engine, still a Pegasus 11 but with complete anti-corrosion protection and an uprated gearbox drive for a 15kVA alternator to supply the greater electrical loads. To facilitate checking engine thrust prior to launch it was planned to add a hold-back link to the main gear, secured to a hydraulic snubber below deck and severed by the pilot via a release button on the nozzle lever, but this was never fitted.

The aircraft nose, however, is totally new, and aesthetically vastly improved. The chief alterations are addition of a multimode radar, installation of a totally different nav/attack system, and accommodation of the extra avionics and cockpit panels by raising the entire cockpit 11in (279mm), which automatically improves pilot view. Cockpit displays were completely redesigned.

Never before had so much mission capability been built into so small an aircraft, and this is combined with the ability to operate from almost any warship, in any weather, with only one man on board and with no external assistance or ground power supplies. The avionics were therefore a major challenge, and the result has proved to be an excellent compromise that has scarcely needed any alteration.

Blue Fox radar

As it is by far the largest sensor, the radar can be dealt with first. Ferranti was the logical supplier, because of its major involvement with the RAF Harrier and its work on the P.1154 radar. In fact the Blue Fox radar was derived more nearly from the Seaspray fitted to Navy Lynx helicopters, but considerably augmented. Operating in I-band, it is a neat modular 186lb (84kg) package, aircooled and installed in a nose which hinges 180° to the left to reduce aircraft length. There are four main mission operating modes: search, with a B-type (sector) scan, PPI, multi-bar (raster) or single scan; attack, with intercept and lead/pursuit or chase in the air-combat mission, and weapon-aiming via the HUD in anti-ship or surface attack; boresight, for quick ranging on targets of opportunity; and xpdr (transponder) for immediate identification of friendly targets. Two two-seat Hunters were rebuilt as T.8M radar trials aircraft, later serving with a third conversion as Sea Harrier radar trainers at Yeovilton. A P.1127(RAF), XV277, was flown in 1974 with a metal mock-up nose. While this was satisfactory aerodynamically, it would not have been adequate to house the desired radar dish. This was the factor that drove the Kingston designers to adopt the raised cockpit configuration.

Left: One of the first ski-jump takeoffs by a Sea Harrier FRS.1 in early 1980 from the newly commissioned HMS *Invincible*, whose ramp is limited to 7° by the location of the Sea Dart SAM launcher (seen, unloaded, on the left). The aircraft has two tanks and three practice bomb carriers.

The nav/attack system installed in the Sea Harrier bears little resemblance to that of the Harrier. It reflects the ship-based environment, which, for example, imposes inertial alignment problems, and the unusual spread of missions. Two digital computers are used, one 20k (20,000 words) WAC (weapon-aiming computer) associated with the HUD and used to provide symbology and weapon-aiming graphics, and an 8k navigation computer which ties together that series of equipments and feeds a nav control/display panel on the right console. Navigation inputs come from: a Ferranti all-attitude TGP (twin-gyro platform) which, while avoiding most INS problems, provides a continuous measure of aircraft attitude and acceleration; a Decca 72 doppler radar and Sperry flux valve, which provide independent ground speed and heading inputs and monitor the TGP; and Tacan, UHF homing, an I-band transponder and an ADC (air-data computer). Even at sea the system takes only 2min to align, and provides: present position as a lat/long or tactical grid reference; range, bearing, course-to-steer and time to any of ten waypoints (any of which can be assigned a velocity, because it might be a ship); estimates of time remaining on task, derived from fuel contents and flow-meter readings; range/bearing to a Tacan station or an offset position; groundspeed/track and wind-speed and direction; and immediate update by pilot input by overflying a known waypoint, radar fix or Tacan.

Above: British Aerospace Dynamics is now in production with the Sea Eagle long-range anti-ship missile, two early examples of which were flown on the first Sea Harrier, XZ438, during carry trials in 1981.

An improved cockpit

Designing the cockpit to accommodate an exceptional amount of display information in a small space was a real challenge, but it has proved popular with pilots and very easy to learn. Thanks to the raised position, the side consoles are wider than in the Harrier, yet more panel space has also been provided ahead. The latest miniaturized displays are used, examples being the row of CWS (centralized warning system) lights around the coaming. The HUD is newer than that of the GR.3, with a larger display linked to the programmable computer interfacing with numerous weapon-aiming and navaid equipments. On return to the ship the approach and landing are assisted by MEL Madge (microwave aircraft digital guidance equipment) which can feed through the WAC to the HUD. The main radar display is to the right, and the pilot has a hand controller at the rear on the left console.

Not only does the seat's elevated position give a better all-round view, but the canopy is bulged at the sides. View to the rear compares favourably with that in any other fighter, and with gear extended the pilot can look across the inlet ducts and check the outrigger gears, which cannot be seen in a GR.3. The seat itself is the latest Martin-Baker type, the Mk 10H, one of the rocket-assisted zero/zero variety (usable at zero height and zero airspeed), and its main parachute is deployed in 1·5s, compared with 2.25s for the Mk 9D of the GR.3. Ahead of the flat bulletproof windscreen is a yaw vane, centred instead of offset as in the GR.3, and the reconnaissance and strike camera is relocated to look out of the right side of the nose. Another addition is a radar

Left: A Sea Harrier cockpit. On the right side of the main panel the radar display (here blanked off for security reasons) replaces the engine/fuel instruments of the GR.3, and basic flight instruments occupy the central area which in the GR.3 is filled by the moving-map display.

British Aerospace Sea Harrier FRS.1

Below: Artwork showing stores normally carried by the Sea Harrier. Item No 8, the reconnaissance pod, could easily be carried, as it is by RAF Harriers, but is not currently required by the Royal Navy. Several other stores could readily be cleared for use.

1 Matra 550 Magic AAM (used by Indian Navy)
2 AIM-9L Sidewinder AAM
3 AIM-9B Sidewinder AAM
4 Sea Eagle ASM
5 Harpoon ASM
6 100gal tank (190gal, 864lit, is now used)
7 Lepus flare
8 Reconnaissance pod
9 30mm Aden gun pod
10 30mm ammunition
11 1,000lb (454kg) GP bomb
12 Matra retarded bomb
13 ML twin carrier with Matra 155 launchers
14 RN 2in (50·8mm) rocket launcher
15 BL.755 cluster bomb

Above: Three-view drawing of a BAe Sea Harrier FRS.1. The position of the nosecone containing the Blue Fox radar main unit when folded back is shown in dotted outline.

Right: Elements of the Ferranti Blue Fox multimode radar, with the mechanically steered aerial (antenna) mounted in its yellow transport cradle. In front are the cockpit push-button and pistol-grip hand controllers.

Below: A selection of stores carried by Sea Harriers. Inboard wing stations have a maximum capacity of 2,000lb (907kg), twice that of the outboard stations.

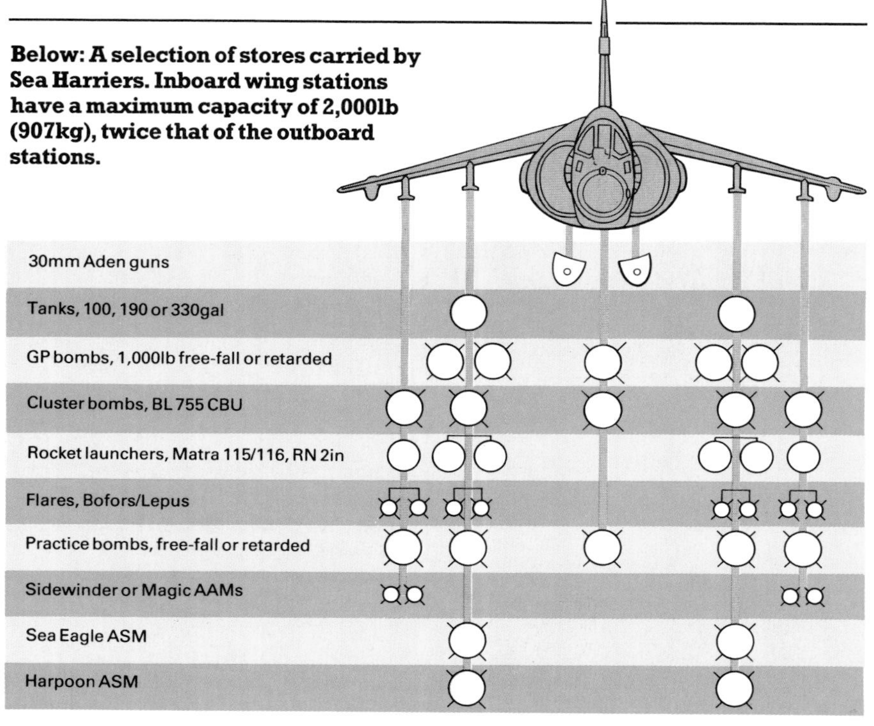

altimeter, with display prominent on the main primary panel fed by aerials recessed in the ventral fin similar to those of the AV-8C.

RWR and armament generally is the same as for the GR.3, though the pylons were strengthened. Weapons, however, have always been different and more diverse, including Sidewinder AAMs, RN 2in (50·8mm) rocket pods and anti-ship missiles. No wiring is provided for a reconnaissance pod.

The original plan was to go ahead with the 24 production aircraft, but in May 1978 the plan was changed, ten additional Sea Harriers being ordered and the first three being earmarked as special trials aircraft (XZ438-440). Because of the complexity of their instrumentation, these aircraft were overtaken by XZ450, the first of what had become 31 production aircraft, and despite delays due to industrial unrest this flew in its primer paint on 20 August 1978. Two weeks later, in Fleet Air Arm livery, it did ski jumps from a new 15° sagging-catenary ramp built by Royal Engineers at the Farnborough airshow using standard Fairey MGB (medium girder bridge) components. The first instrumented aircraft, XZ438, flew on 30 December 1978, and subsequent progress was rapid. XZ451, with Modex number 100, was delivered to RNAS Yeovilton on 18 June 1979, the IFTU (Intensive Flying Trials Unit), No 700A Sqn, commissioned there on 19 September, and a month later an extremely successful sea trials programme was flown from HMS *Hermes* in the Irish Sea.

Subsequently 700A became 899 Harrier HQ Sqn, with Nos 800 and 801 Sqns as the combat units, the plan being to assign one to each Command Cruiser: *Invincible, Illustrious* and *Ark Royal*. By sheer chance it was decided to retain the old carrier *Hermes* for Sea Harrier training, despite a decision to send her to the breakers' yard in 1982 on the commissioning of *Illustrious*. After much argument it was decided to carry out a refit in late 1979 and fit her with a 12° ski ramp. How momentous this narrow decision would be, could not be dreamed of.

Overseas sales

Subsequent RN work-up of the Sea Harriers is discussed in the next chapter. Meanwhile, navies around the world continued to watch the progress of these unique aircraft with growing interest. India remained at the top of the list of serious potential customers, and Australia planned to buy HMS *Invincible* in 1983 (though remaining undecided about fast V/STOL jets). The first customer to follow the RN's lead did, in fact, turn out to be India, which had long used Hawker (Armstrong Whitworth) Sea Hawks from INS *Vikrant*. In July 1972 John Farley flew the company demo two-seater, G-VTOL, to give requested demonstrations from the ageing carrier despite the 30°C steamy monsoon atmosphere. Farley flew 22 times in two days, and, when he left, the Indian Navy was totally sold on this amazing aircraft. It placed an order for six Sea Harrier Mk 51 single-seaters, and two two-seat Mk 60s, for delivery in 1983.

During the Falklands war the Indian

Left: XZ492 of No 800 Sqn flying over HMS *Hermes* in 1981, with AIM-9B Sidewinders, tanks and guns. At that time *Hermes* was earmarked for immediate scrapping; nobody could foresee how vital she would later be.

Navy team at British Aerospace watched for a sudden speed-up on their aircraft, indicating that they were being rushed through for delivery to the Royal Navy instead. This never happened, and the first Mk 51, bearing the white tiger badge of No 300 Squadron, was handed over at Dunsfold on 27 January 1983. Pilots and ground staff were trained at Yeovilton before the first FRS.51s flew out to *Vikrant* in late-1983. Differences between the Mk 51 and the RN FRS.1 are minor; for example a gaseous oxygen system is fitted, and the AAM is the Matra Magic.

Today the Sea Harrier is not only a formidable and exceptionally versatile warplane but it has been proved so in unusually tough circumstances. In the longer term it will require updating, and though there is every indication that the airframe will need little attention, BAe has given the question of an MLU (mid-life update) prolonged consideration and come up with a comprehensive package which it is expected will be funded for incorporation in the late 1980s. The basic aircraft might receive several AV-8B-type changes including zero-scarf front nozzles, LERX for combat agility, detail changes to improve aerodynamics and STO lift, and increased internal fuel. In the nose will be a new and more advanced radar, funded by the MoD from Ferranti's private-venture Blue Falcon, with all the expected features of a high-power pulse doppler set, including: look-up/look-down; improved combat performance at high altitude; TWS (track while scanning); segregation of multiple targets; and allocation of threat priorities. New wing-tip launchers will be added for AIM-9L, later replaced by the European Asraam (advanced short-range AAM), while the wing pylons may be tailored to single or paired AIM-120A (Amraam, advanced medium-range AAM), which will give a stand-off "fire and forget" kill capability. Other changes may include an Obogs (on-board oxygen generating system) and an internal EW installation as in the updated RAF GR.3.

Above: XZ457, aircraft "713" of 899 Sqn at Yeovilton, destroyed two Mirages and a Skyhawk but is seen here over Somerset in company with a newly-acquired Harrier T.4(RN), the Royal Navy's two-seat trainer version.

Left: Now intensively used by the Indian Navy's No 300 Sqn, IN601, the first Sea Harrier FRS.51, is seen here in primer paint and temporary SBAC registration G-9-478 on its first flight on 6 August 1982. A month later it was at the Farnborough Air Show (see above).

Above: Externally there are few differences between the Indian Navy FRS.51 and the regular FRS.1, apart from the white tiger badge of 300 Sqn. Internally a gaseous oxygen system is fitted, and the Indian Navy's AAM is the Matra 550 Magic.

Operation Corporate

The recovery of the Falkland Islands from the occupying forces of Argentina was quite unlike any other campaign in the history of human conflict. Operation Corporate was mounted at very short notice, and involved all the armed forces of the Crown in a land/sea/air war utterly unlike anything for which those forces had been trained, and in a remote and inhospitable part of the globe some 4,000 miles from the nearest friendly base! The success of the entire operation depended upon the Sea Harrier, later joined by the RAF Harrier, both of which at the start were unproven weapon systems.

Above: Unusually approaching from dead astern, a Sea Harrier recovers aboard *Hermes* at twilight. One Sidewinder has been fired, but tanks are retained. All touchdowns are vertical.

The refusal of a group of Argentine scrap-metal dealers to leave British territory on South Georgia gave a clue that a direct confrontation was possible, and on 31 March 1982 Admiral Sir John Fieldhouse RN, who had just returned to Britain from Exercise Springtrain in the Mediterranean, was ordered to begin preparing Task Force 317, of which he was to be overall Commander. Indeed, he had ordered Rear-Admiral "Sandy" Woodward to prepare a detachment before he left Gibraltar. Immediately plans were put into action involving all the fighting services.

Crucial to the possible retaking of the islands was airpower, because Argentina possessed powerful fighter and attack brigades within both its air force and naval aviation. Thanks to the decision of the British government in 1966 there was no seagoing British airpower whatsoever, except for the small force of Sea Harriers, which had barely settled down and whose pilots were mostly inexperienced. Even this force had only come into existence in the teeth of opposition from defence officials and the Treasury.

At RNAS Yeovilton, Somerset, were the three Sea Harrier squadrons: 800 (Lt-Cdr Andy Auld), 801 (Lt-Cdr Nigel Ward) and the HQ unit 899 (Lt-Cdr Tony Ogilvy). To make things more difficult, 801 were on leave on the day of mobilization (2 April) and 800 were due to go on leave at mid-day! Each had an establishment of five aircraft, but 899 was split up to augment the two first-line squadrons, so that on 5 April, with spare aircraft added to the establishment, HMS *Hermes*, the Task Force flagship, sailed from Portsmouth with 11 Sea Harriers of 800 Sqn which had landed on an already overcrowded deck, and a few miles out a 12th landed on. The brand-new HMS *Invincible* was almost as crowded, and among her air units was 801 Sqn with eight aircraft. Among the mountains of stores, all loaded in less than three days but which were to sustain a campaign lasting three months, were the newest and best Sidewinder AAMs, the AIM-9L. Not previously used by the RN, though in production by a European industrial group, AIM-9L has a completely new guidance system, more powerful control fins and a high-power warhead.

Above: An aircraft of No 800 Sqn on the slippery deck of *Hermes* in a force 10 gale. In the background are the flagship's "goalkeeper" (*Broadsword*) and, on the skyline, *Invincible*.

The unknown quantity

Thus, from the start, the Task Force had a small air component equipped with a unique aircraft which, though it was relatively new and untested in battle, promised to be outstandingly versatile. In particular, it was expected to be able to intercept and destroy attacking Argentine aircraft, including the Mach 2 Mirage and Dagger – all are called Mirages here, for simplicity – which in low-level attack are extremely subsonic. By an accident of geography the Falklands are at such a distance from the several large mainland airbases that, while low-level attacks by the Argentine aircraft were perfectly capable of being mounted, there would not be a lot of fuel to spare, especially if afterburner was used. At the same time, the Task Force was going to stand off at a considerable distance, and the Sea Harriers likewise were not going to have much time on station either. Not least, the Argentine aircraft were several times more numerous. Put another way, the total embarked force of 20 British fixed-wing aircraft was so small that even a single combat loss was going to be significant.

At an early stage it was clear that more aircraft would be needed. There were other Sea Harriers and pilots, and there were also the Harriers of the RAF, and preparations were made to bring as many into the South Atlantic as the two flat-top ships could accommodate. Lt-Cdr Gedge was ordered to form a third Sea Harrier squadron, and he immediately located Sea Harriers at Boscombe, Dunsfold and other locations, though none was in front-line condition and almost all were in various stages of refit, rebuild, special trials or still being completed by the maker. All were urgently hurried through to the latest combat-ready state – without, incidentally, commandeering a single one of the FRS.51 aircraft building for the Indian Navy. Lt-Cdr Gedge just managed to scrape together an adequate number of Sea Harrier pilots, including some on exchange posting in Australia and the USA. By April 30 Gedge had formed 809 Sqn, though he had to import two RAF

Below: This profile shows XV787, first flown on 9 September 1970 and heavily engaged on combat missions with 1(F) Sqn in the Falklands in 1982. Note the chin transponder and Paveway LGB.

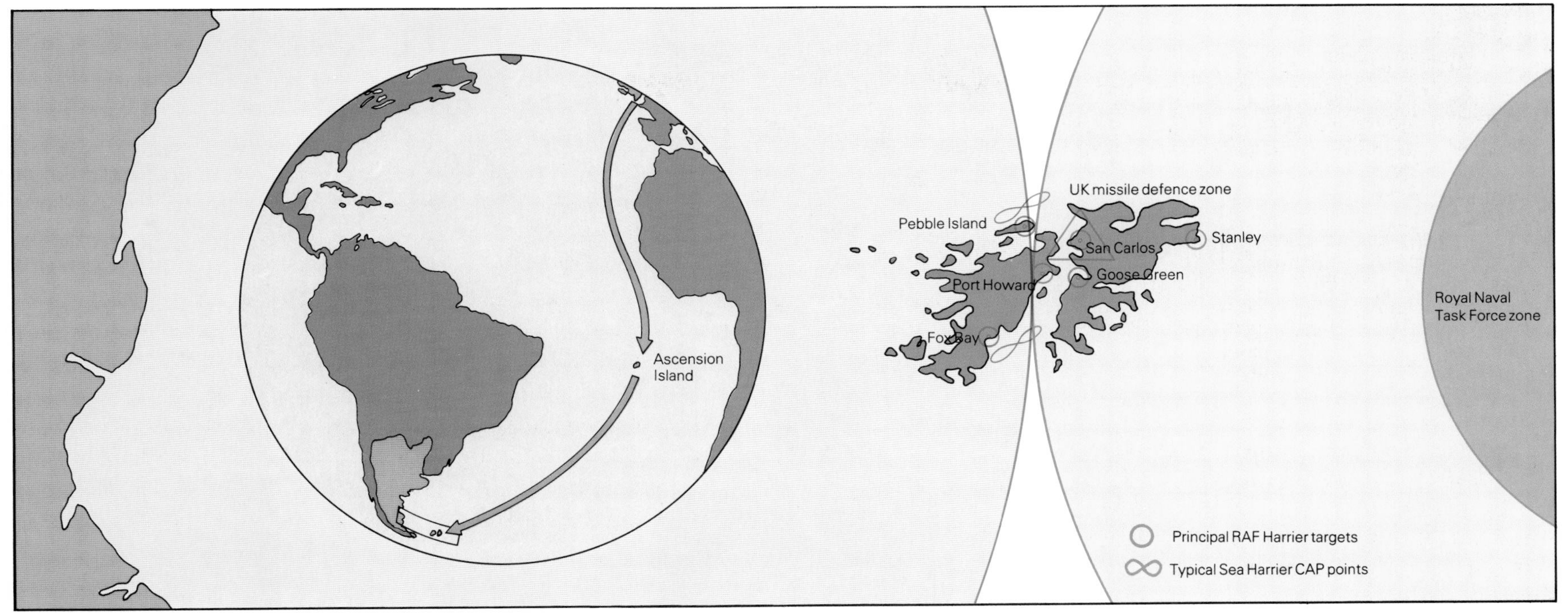

Above: An overall idea of the geography is provided by these two maps, one of the globe superimposed on a larger-scale map of the Falklands. The former emphasizes the colossal distance from Britain, as far as New York to New Zealand. The local map shows a 400 nautical mile radius from Argentina in red and a 200 nm radius from the Task Force in blue.

Right: Sea Harrier XZ498 of No 800 Sqn makes a VL aboard *Illustrious* in Falklands waters in 1983. During the war she served with 801 on *Invincible*.

Harrier pilots who had Lightning interceptor experience, and he also had to leave two aircraft behind to carry on essential development and training.

The eight aircraft of the new squadron were to a slightly later standard than other Sea Harriers, and they later had twin Sidewinder launchers and 190gal (864lit) tanks. They were factory-painted in a shade of light "barley" grey which RAE experts calculated would blend in best with winter South Atlantic environments. The other squadrons had left Britain painted in standard dark sea grey with white undersides, with bold unit insignia on the tails. Clearly they had to be toned down for warfare, and the decision was taken to paint the undersides the same colour as the top, to apply Type B (red/blue) roundels and low-contrast black serial number and Modex numbers, and no other markings. The repainting was done on the journey south. *Invincible*'s modern air-conditioning enabled spray-painting to be used but in *Hermes* 800 Sqn had to be laboriously painted by hand.

Back at Yeovilton No 809 readied itself for combat, the two hijacked RAF pilots quickly learning how to use the Blue Fox radar and launch over a ski jump. The flight-refuelling probes were fitted, and on 31 April/1 May the whole squadron flew out to Ascension Island. All aircraft refuelled a total of 14 times from Victors, though few pilots had ever made an AAR (air/air refuelling) contact before. As in all such deployments the objective was to keep all tanks nearly filled, so that, if the next refuelling were to fail for any

reason, the aircraft could still fly to a friendly airbase. At Ascension the newly formed squadron parked awaiting a ship, and every possible crevice and hole was taped over to keep out the wind-blown volcanic grit and sand.

By Easter, 3 April, the decision had been taken to commit RAF No 1 Sqn (W/C Peter Squire), with the Harrier GR.3, but in this case much remained to be done. The prime mission was expected to be air defence, for which the RAF Harrier units were initially neither trained nor equipped. Many aircraft modifications were required, and as with the RN units the situation was compounded by the squadron's planned imminent departure for a major exercise in Canada. S/L Bob Iveson, a No 1 Sqn flight commander, was sent to Liverpool to study a large and fast container ship, *Atlantic Conveyor*, and report on her suitability as a Harrier ferry. It was clear she could carry the aircraft as deck cargo, but no flying would appear possible, and there were major problems with personnel accommodation.

She had been laid-up at Liverpool, but was quickly readied, and while still at Liverpool a Sea Harrier carried out deck trials; but she had to sail, jammed with stores, on 23 April without any fixed-wing aircraft aboard. By this time the Harriers, 14 in number, had already been substantially modified. The largest task was to insert along the wings the wiring for Sidewinders on the outer pylons. Launch rails for these missiles were added, and the complete installation was tested with live firings from Llanbedr on the Aberporth range. In the interest of ordnance commonality the aircraft was cleared to use the RN rocket launcher, housing 36 rockets of 2in (50·4mm) calibre instead of the usual RAF Matra 115 which takes 18 (or 19 if the centre tube is used) of 68mm. Another new weapon cleared in a hurry was the Mk 13/18 Paveway II LGB (laser-guided bomb), which was thought to be particularly appropriate to the GR.3 since this aircraft has a compatible 10·6 micron laser. Under the nose a blister appeared covering a transponder added to enhance the GR.3's response to the ship aircraft direction radars. Also to be cleared for use were the big 330gal (1500lit) drop tanks, which were to be needed on the long flight south.

A "marinised" GR.3

Apart from these modifications, all the GR.3s were put through an environmental protection programme, as many holes and joints as possible being sealed to prevent salt-water ingress even if waves were to break over the aircraft. Where ingestion could not be prevented, new drain holes were provided. Lashing-down lugs were added to the outrigger gears, and other changes were made to facilitate shipboard operation. Meanwhile, Ferranti Ltd had worked around the clock updating Finrae (Ferranti inertial rapid-alignment equipment) to ready the GR.3's INS immediately prior to each mission. The trolley-mounted package was based on the FIN 1064 (updated Jaguar) INS, and continuously provided north and horizontal references over long periods. Three Finraes were flown to Ascension and taken aboard *Atlantic Conveyor*, and the final software program was sent via communications satellite direct to the South Atlantic.

It had been planned for each pilot of No 1 Sqn to qualify by making three takeoffs over the ski ramp at Yeovilton, but it was evident after a few attempts that there was "nothing to it", and a single launch apiece was sufficient. Close air combat was another matter, and every pilot put in intensive DACT (dissimilar air-combat training), including air combat against Mirages of l'Armée de l'Air and Super Etendards of l'Aéronavale. Then the first group of nine Harriers flew from Wittering to St Mawgan, Cornwall, and from there went on to Ascension on 3-5 May. Each was met five times by Victors, the procedures again providing for diversion to a friendly base should the next AAR fail to top up because of malfunction. Typical flight time was 9h 15min, easily a record for any Harrier in RAF service. Not for the first time the RAF resolved to rethink the traditional "relief tube" and rubber bottle, with a Velcro slit in the immersion suit.

At Ascension three of the aircraft were temporarily commandeered to provide local air defence. The other six air-taxied across to the moored *Atlantic Conveyor*, each making a VL on the newly added VTOL spot in the bows, then turning aft and taxiing down a narrow canyon left between walls of two-high containers – which provided the only protection against the sea – to a

Above: A tradesman of RAF No 1(F) Sqn together with the pilot use the Finrae to align the inertial platform of a Harrier GR.3 prior to a sortie from HMS *Hermes* in May 1982. The Sea Harrier in the rear had different navaids and did not need Finrae.

Below: *Atlantic Conveyor* steaming south in early May 1982, with six Harriers and eight Sea Harriers. Only the former really needed the protective bags, and one Sea Harrier of 809 was parked fully fuelled and armed on the bow spot.

marshalled spot, where the aircraft were parked and wrapped in Driclad envelopes. Few of the pilots had been aboard a ship before. The ship also took aboard the eight Sea Harriers of 809 Sqn, and various helicopters. The final Sea Harrier was parked at readiness on the VTOL spot, for local defence. On 18 May *Atlantic Conveyor* passed lat 52°S and closed with the Task Force, whereupon the GR.3s, freed from their garments, air-taxied across to *Hermes*. This time their pilots experienced a deck pitching and rolling in what were soon to be recognized as normal South Atlantic conditions. Meanwhile 809 put six aircraft on *Hermes* and two on *Invincible*, though later this squadron had four on each ship as planned.

In late May five more GR.3s, completing No 1's total of 14, were flown out to Ascension. Four were taken aboard the *Contender Bezant*, a Ro-Ro ship whose conversion had caused major problems. The remaining aircraft, plus the three now released from defending Ascension, flew all the way south to the Task Force, one pair on 1 June and the other pair on 8 June. This time the landlubber pilots viewed 4,000 miles (6440km) of cold ocean with anxiety. There was no question of there being any possibility of diversion to any land base whatsoever, and for the last 800 nautical miles (1500km) they were entirely alone, and though they could use Tacan they had to preserve radio silence. To cap it all, one pair arrived on the deck of *Hermes* in the middle of an Argentine air attack.

On its way south the original Task Force had launched CAPs (combat air patrols) with increasing frequency. These ranged out as far as 120 miles (193km), usually to the south-west, and as the TEZ (the 200-mile, 322km Total Exclusion Zone) was approached a lot of flying was done at night. In any case, with the onset of winter, daylight gradually shortened to a narrow band between about 1100 and 1730 local time, and weather progressively worsened. Much of the hardest action, in late May and June, took place with gale-force winds, mountainous seas, and everything on deck being covered in condensation which froze at night. Towards the middle of June it snowed heavily. For much of the time cloud base was at 200ft (90m) and occasionally it was half this, with visibility typically being half a mile (800m) with high winds. Under these conditions the Harriers and Sea Harriers experienced no special difficulty, whereas conventional carrier-based aircraft in a similar situation would not have been able to fly at all.

Meeting the "Argies"

Contact with what had become the enemy was made on 25 April when a Sea Harrier of 801 intercepted an FAA (Fuerza Aérea Argentina) 707 on long-range reconnaissance looking for the Task Force. It was outside the TEZ and, the rules of engagement at that time being restrictive, it was not attacked.

The first combat missions were flown by 12 aircraft from *Hermes* at dawn on 1 May. With top cover provided by 801 from *Invincible*, nine Sea Harriers made a carefully planned low-level attack on Port Stanley airfield, which had been bombed on the previous night by a Vulcan. The first four came in at 520kt (963km/h) at 100ft (30m) with variously fuzed 1,000lb (454kg) bombs to hit the SAM and gun defences, attacking in a forwards toss. This went well, the air-burst weapons being seen to explode directly over their targets. Four of the other five aircraft each had three BL.755 cluster bombs, for use against aircraft and support areas, while the fifth had three 1,000lb (454kg) with contact fuzes. All aircraft also had two tanks and the gun pods. Despite intense ground fire, only one aircraft was hit, taking a 20mm shell through the fin. The holes were quickly repaired with Speedtape (adhesive-backed aluminium tape). The three other Sea Harriers from *Hermes* hit Goose Green, again encountering intense hostile fire.

During the daylight hours of 1 May several pairs of 801's Sea Harriers encountered Mirages, at least three of which very inexpertly fired semi-active Matra R.530 AAMs at long range, all of which were evaded by the RN aircraft. The CO of 801, Lt-Cdr Ward, frustratingly chased three T-34C Turbo Mentors on FAC duty through low cloud without managing to nail one. But later on that day 801 launched two aircraft to intercept a high-altitude raid and met at least two Mirages head-on. Lt Steve Thomas used his radar to control the two aircraft into firing positions, while two enemy missiles zipped harmlessly over his cockpit. F/Lt Paul Barton, RAF, then let go a locked-on AIM-9L and saw his target disappear in a fireball, which was the invariable result of a -9L strike. A few seconds later Thomas also got into firing parameters and probably bagged the other Mirage, but it entered dense cloud with the -9L chasing it. At dusk Lt Alan Curtis and Lt-Cdr Mike Broadwater carried out a textbook autonomous radar interception of two Canberras, scoring one confirmed and one probable. The day was rounded off by *Hermes*, which launched two aircraft against another high raid. Again the enemy opened fire at long range, the Sea Harrier evading the missile, and the second Sea Harrier,

Left: On 8 June 1982 Marshall of Cambridge flew the first C.1(K) tanker version of the RAF Hercules, which can operate from Stanley. Here a "Herc tanker" refuels an RAF Harrier GR.3 over the South Atlantic in 1983.

Below: Hosing down the flight deck of the Task Force flagship shortly after the Argentine surrender, when the worst of the blizzards were over. In the theatre all Sea Harriers on *Hermes* were administered by 800 Sqn.

Above: **Flying practice continued on the journey south in April 1982. Ready for the first real mission aboard *Hermes* are 1,000lb retarded bombs, AIM-9Ls and Mk 46 AS torpedoes for the ship's Sea King HAS.5 helicopters.**

Harrier Force Deployed

Sea Harrier	Harrier GR.3	Method of Transit
12	0	Embarked in UK, HMS *Hermes*
8	0	Embarked in UK, HMS *Invincible*
8	6	Flown UK to Ascension Island, embarked *Atlantic Conveyor*
0	4	Flown UK to Ascension Island, flown to 52°S, vertical landing on HMS *Hermes*
28	**10**	**Total**
0	4	Flown UK to Ascension Island, embarked *Contender Bezant*, flown off to Port Stanley having arrived after ceasefire

Harrier Force Missions

Sorties	2,000+ South of Ascension Island
	1,650 within Total Exclusion Zone
Combat Missions	**Sea Harrier:**
	1,100+ CAP sorties
	90 offensive support
	GR.3:
	125 ground attack and tactical reconnaissance
Flying Rate	approx 55 hours/aircraft/month
	up to 10 sorties/aircraft/day
	3-4 sorties/pilot/day
	up to 10 hours/day in cockpit
Pilot/aircraft ratio	1.2 initially
	1.4 later
Aircraft availability at beginning of each day	95%
Operational loss rate/sortie	0.38%
Overall loss rate/sortie	0.61%
Known successful ejection attempts	100%

again flown by an RAF officer on exchange, F/Lt Bertie Penfold, bagged a Mirage with a -9L.

Few days were to be as busy as this, and losses began with Lt Nick Taylor, who was killed by AAA at Goose Green on 4 May. By mid-May the Sea Harriers had completely covered the islands with photo reconnaissance, and on 20 May the first RAF Harriers also got into action. The pilots of No 1 Sqn were, on the whole, far more experienced in low-level attack missions, and though they had looked forward to flying air defence sorties, the Royal Navy took the view that this was best left to the Sea Harriers. It was therefore decided that the GR.3s should be rewired to carry offensive stores outboard and they subsequently took over most of the low-level attack and reconnaissance, leaving the Sea Harriers to fly CAP and other air-defence duties.

GR.3s join in

Prior to the arrival of the GR.3s the Sea Harrier pilots had decided to fly attack missions by day and night using a mix of medium level bombing and low-level tosses. The RAF Harriers worked almost exclusively at the lowest possible level, and, because even with the help of the surviving Finrae (two went down with the sunk *Atlantic Conveyor*) navigational accuracies could not quite equal those achieved with stationary alignment on an airfield, it was decided to navigate and attack visually wherever possible.

The first mission by No 1 Sqn, tasked on 20 May, was a strike against fuel and oil dumps at Fox Bay. Led by the CO, with both his flight commanders, S/Ls Bob Iveson and Jerry Pook, the tight formation made a single pass at low level straight over the target and used BL.755 CBUs (cluster bomb units). There were many secondary explosions, culminating in a giant fireball. Subsequently the GR.3s flew 125 sorties on attack and reconnaissance, the latter using the centreline pod. Three aircraft were lost, all due to ground defensive fire, which was usually intense and caused so much aircraft damage as to depress serviceability below the amazing figure of "above 99.9 per cent" set by the Sea Harriers.

The three losses were: XZ963, 21 May, hit by Blowpipe missile at Goose Green, F/Lt Jeffrey Glover ejected and captured (the only British PoW); XZ998, 27 May, hit by two large-calibre shells when at high speed at below 100ft supporting 2 Para near Goose Green, S/L Iveson losing flight control and hydraulic pressure, the aircraft then catching fire, arresting dive by vectoring nozzles but finally having to eject, evading capture and being picked up by Royal Marine flying Army Gazelle over two days later; XZ972, 30 May, after flying through heavy fire on 19 previous missions took several hits at low level when attacking a helicopter landing site west of Stanley and began losing fuel rapidly, and though S/L Pook thought his chance of survival poor because of loss of radio he was in fact accompanied by his wingman who had alerted *Hermes*, and when Pook ejected 45 miles (72km) short of the ship he actually heard the Sea King that was waiting to collect him.

Pook was only off operations for one day, because of a stiff neck, and in the closing stages he was one of the GR.3 pilots to use smart LGBs against difficult point targets. The hills around Port Stanley enabled all such attacks to be made behind cover, the Harrier approaching on the far side of Mounts Harriet, Tumbledown, or Two Sisters and lobbing the weapon in a toss over the summit. On two occasions the FAC (forward air controller) fired the Ferranti designator too soon and the LGB failed to achieve lock, but on all other FAC-designated smart attacks there was a direct hit. This weapon would have been valuable on many earlier attacks, almost all of which were against small targets that were exceedingly difficult to locate, but it might have been difficult to set up a friendly designator and a good launch trajectory. On at least one occasion, over Stanley airfield, an LGB failed to lock-on when designated by a GR.3's own laser. On some occasions attacks on heavily defended point targets were made at just above ground level by groups of GR.3s directed by a Sea Harrier overhead at much higher altitude who could see the target and send minor course changes.

In the whole of Operation Corporate the RN Sea Harriers flew 2,376 missions for a total of 2,675·4 hours. Seldom, if ever, has so much depended on so few aircraft. Despite the appalling weather, aircraft averaged 55 hours per month, flying 6 to 10 sorties per day. It was common for pilots to fly two combat missions without leaving the cockpit, and the serviceability never fell below 95 per cent. HMS *Invincible*'s aircraft flew 99.97 per cent of the tasked sorties, losing only

Confirmed Sea Harrier Kills

Aircraft	AIM-9L Sidewinder	30mm guns	Total
Mirage	11	0	11
A-4 Skyhawk	6	2	8
Canberra	1	0	1
Pucará	0	1	1
C-130 Hercules	½	½	1
Puma helicopter	0	0	1*
Total	**18½**	**3½**	**23**

*Hit ground during evasive action

Confirmed Kills on Ground

	Aircraft	30mm guns	Cluster bomb	Total
Sea Harrier	A-109	1	0	1
	Islander	0	1	1
	Pucará	0	1	1
	Puma	2	0	2
Harrier GR.3	Chinook	1	0	1
	Puma	2	1	3
Total		**6**	**3**	**9**

Harrier Force Losses

Reason	Sea Harrier	Harrier GR.3
Air-to-Air combat	0	0
Ground Defences	2	3
Slid off deck	1	0
Hit sea after take-off	1	0
Collided or flew into sea	2	0
Total	**6**	**3**

Right: Sea Harrier development aircraft XZ440 was used for the urgent clearance of the 190gal (864lit) drop tank and the twin Sidewinder AAM launcher, here loaded with the newly available AIM-9L.

part of one sortie through unserviceability. Operations continued at a high intensity in conditions far below peacetime limits, and were assisted by local extensions given to various component lives, including the complete engine, and by allowing interchange between Harrier and Sea Harrier engines and fuel system components.

After the shock of meeting the Sea Harrier on 1 May, the Argentine FAA and CANA (naval air arm) avoided any clash with "the Black Death" for three weeks. Despite this, there was no let-up in round-the-clock CAPs, and sadly two aircraft, XZ452 and 453, flown by Lt-Cdr John Eyton-Jones and Lt Alan Curtis, disappeared on 6 May while on CAP in very bad weather; almost certainly they collided in cloud. On 24 May ZA192 hit the sea shortly after takeoff on a stormy night, Lt-Cdr G. W. J. Batt being killed. On 29 May ZA174 slid off the rolling icy deck of HMS *Invincible* while moving forward for the next takeoff; Lt-Cdr Mike Broadwater ejected and was picked up by a Sea King. The sixth and last loss was on 1 June when 801's air-warfare instructor, F/Lt Ian Mortimer, RAF, was shot down by a SAM while at 15,000ft (4572m) in XZ456. Mortimer was snatched from under the noses of the enemy in an amazing night search/rescue mission lasting nine hours.

During the lull in enemy air activity, 800 Sqn knocked out the reconnaissance trawler *Narwhal* on 9 May, and just a week later crippled the supply ship *Bahia Buen Suceso* and damaged the *Rio Carcarana*. On 22 May a patrol boat was strafed and forced to beach. By this time the RAF Harriers were flying the bulk of the attack missions – to the RAF's disgust because, though it had shown antipathy towards air combat when specifying the Harrier in the 1960s, it now naturally wanted a share of the air combat glory.

"Black Death" dominant

This continued to be cornered by the Navy, which had many brief but intense combats. All hell was let loose on 21 May (which happened to be Argentine Navy Day) at the start of the British assault landings. No. 800 downed four A-4s with Sidewinders and one with guns on that day, bagged a Mirage on 24 May, and had a particularly good day on 8 June when two of its aircraft splashed a formation of four Mirages: F/Lt Dave Morgan, RAF, getting two, Lt Dave Smith downing one, and the fourth Mirage hitting the sea during evasive action. The detailed analysis of Operation Corporate at first credited Sea Harriers with 20 confirmed and three probable kills, but this was later revised to 23 plus three probable, one of the additions being the C-130.

Above: The Task Force flagship returned to Portmouth on 21 July, to a welcome that was deeply moving. Sea Harriers urgently needed at Yeovilton were flown off from the Bay of Biscay, but six were ranged on deck, together with the entire ship's company.

In late May Nos 11 and 59 Sqns Royal Engineers constructed an FOB (Forward Operating Base) at Port San Carlos. It comprised an 850ft (259m) strip made of MEXE aluminium planking, with taxi and parking loops at one end where fuel was stored in large flexible pillow tanks. The FOB was not used for reloading ordnance, but it enabled Harriers and Sea Harriers to put in almost twice as much time on CAP or cab-rank attack patrol by eliminating the round trip of some 400 miles back to the ship to refuel. One GR.3 sank through a joint in the metal matting, the nose gear going in up to the landing light. Using RE heavy lift gear the aircraft was bodily wrenched free; then it went straight back into action. On another occasion W/C Squire was making the authorized slow approach, with gear down and landing light on to avoid being engaged by British Rapiers, when his jet blast lifted a section of matting which struck his aircraft, XZ989. The impact drove the nozzles to the aft position, and the Harrier hit the ground hard, careered through the strip, severing it, and continued up a nearby hill and over the brow before coming to rest in a Rapier crew's slit trench. The runway was quickly repaired.

Throughout the campaign nobody was more impressed by the performance of the Harrier and Sea Harrier than the men who flew and maintained them. Over 2,000 sorties had been flown, in the harshest conditions imaginable, and each day aircraft availability for both types together averaged better than 95 per cent. Unserviceability lost less than 1·0 per cent of the planned missions, despite the fact that virtually every aircraft took damage from ground fire. Many aircraft, mainly RAF Harriers because of their low attack tasking, took numerous hits from calibres up to 20mm yet were operational on the next day. one GR.3 was hit in the RCV hot-air duct near the tail. On its approach to *Hermes* with nozzles down, the rear end quickly cooked up until it was almost red hot, but XW919 was back in action 36h later; a performance that seems to typify the achievement of these aircraft during this arduous campaign.

Left: Removing the protective nosecap from one of the newly added AIM-9Ls on a GR.3 of No 1(F) Sqn at the forward base at San Carlos. Note the badge of HarDet (Harrier Detachment). Even in operations from this land site the INS was seldom used, aircraft using dead-reckoning and the pilots' eyeballs.

Harrier II

McDonnell Aircraft (MCAIR) of St Louis became associated with the original Hawker V/STOL programme in 1969, with an AV-8A licence agreement which also included the right for the US company to develop derived aircraft using the vectored-thrust principle. With staggering shortsightedness the British government opted out of a collaborative programme in 1975, leaving the next generation to St Louis. The next generation is Harrier II, and most of the production will take place in the United States.

Above: Still obviously a Harrier, the AV-8B Harrier II is at the same time a totally new aeroplane. Sadly for Britain, government policy in 1975 has transferred control to the United States.

By 1971 the Harrier was in production for the RAF and the almost identical AV-8A for the US Marine Corps. Though a few dissenting voices were still heard, which for reasons of ignorance or vested interest claimed that jet V/STOL was not cost/effective, or immature, or merely "foreign", it was obvious to any thinking person that it represented the dawn of a new era in aviation. So Hawker and MCAIR, and Rolls-Royce and Pratt & Whitney, did the obvious and began studying advanced developments of both the Harrier and its Pegasus engine.

Unlike previous aircraft, the Harrier and its Pegasus engine are intimately integrated. Quite apart from the patent situation, no other engine could provide both thrust and lift, and as the future of the Harrier appeared to depend crucially upon the provision of more of both of these factors, the foundation for the Advanced Harrier appeared to be a more powerful Pegasus.

Rolls-Royce Bristol decided to build a demonstrator engine to show the kind of performance possible with a few modifications. The new engine proposed was given the designation Pegasus 15, but the demonstrator was an intermediate engine using the existing Pegasus 11 core and adding only the proposed Pegasus 15 fan, with a diameter increased by 2¼in (57mm) to handle a significantly increased airflow. The Pegasus 15 was aimed at 24,500lb (11 113kg) thrust, so the Bristol team were pleased when the lash-up demo engine gave a figure of 24,900lb (11 295kg) on its first testbed run in May 1972. Hawker and MCAIR felt safe in assuming 25,000lb (11 340kg) in their aircraft studies.

Not least of the encouraging aspects of the Advanced Harrier was that this time there appeared likely to be four major launch customers: the RAF, Royal Navy, US Marine Corps, and US Navy. The latter had decided to deploy a major force of advanced V/STOL fighters aboard its Sea Control Ships, which in many ways were to be like the Royal Navy's *Invincible*. A Joint Management Committee was set up at government level with representatives of the civilian defence ministries (Mintech for Britain), the four customer services and the four main industrial partners. Hawker at Kingston produced the P.1184 and P.1185 project studies. MCAIR produced the AV-8C (not today's AV-8C), a minimum-change Harrier development with a long-span swept wing based on Douglas work with NASA's Richard T. Whitcomb with a supercritical profile matched to Mach 0·92 cruise (and originally studied for a developed DC-9). Such a wing could house more fuel and greatly increase STO lift, besides having enough span for numerous stores pylons. All the studies featured a raised cockpit with all-round view, and of course the inlets had to be enlarged, though it was just posssible to squeeze the Pegasus 15 into the existing size of fuselage.

The AV-16 design

Though Hawker and MCAIR collaborated closely, and had growing technical teams at each other's plants, they pursued their studies independently. By 1973, after agonizing evaluations, it had been decided to let the Pegasus fan grow a further half-inch, to get 25,000lb (11 340kg) with lower turbine temperature and thus achieve long low-cost life, even though this meant a redesign of the fuselage. The AV-8-Plus also introduced a further improved high-airflow elliptical-lip inlet provided with a second row of suck-in auxiliary doors. Both teams also began to discover ways in which local modifications could increase VTO or STO lift without any appreciable penalty. Wisely, both judged that the right course was to modify the proven Harrier as little as possible, and to do so only when a major gain appeared possible with small technical risk. Both adopted the designation AV-16, meaning twice the capability of an AV-8.

Unfortunately, some customers, including both navies, kept harping on the supposed primitive simplicity of the basic Harrier – which in fact is why it has survived and succeeded – and on the apparent advantages for naval missions of a highly supersonic V/STOL. The US Naval Air Systems Command asked both airframe companies how they would design such a machine, and Hawker dusted off its latest series of S (for supersonic) family of studies. These featured a PCB-boosted four-poster engine, of the kind described in the final chapter, which in turn pushed the main gears out into the wing as in the P.1154RN. The wing itself was naturally not only unlike that of a Harrier but utterly unlike that of the AV-8-Plus, which far from yielding

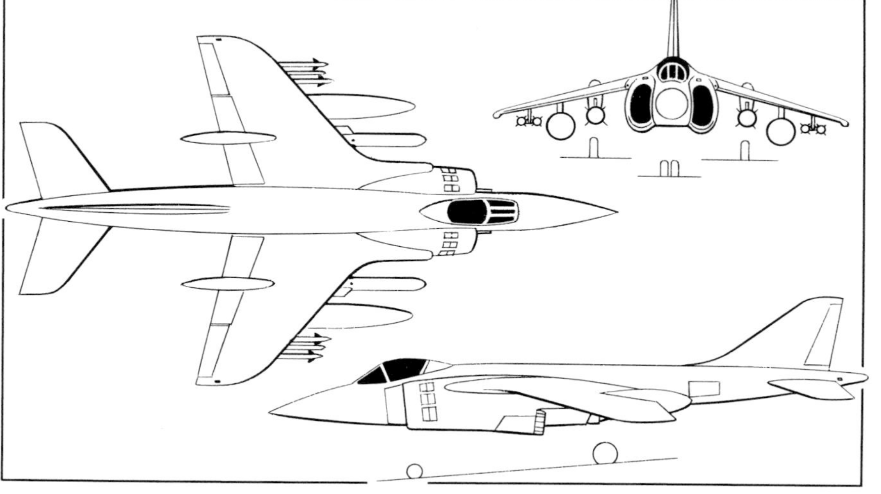

Left: Shown with an assortment of tanks and weapons in the plan and head-on views, the S-6 was one of the "might have been" supersonic designs studied at HSA Kingston in 1973-4.

Below: A direct plan view emphasizes the more obvious new features of the AV-8B, especially the new wing. Low-visibility markings highlight the APU (GTS) inlet and exhaust apertures.

Above: This unusual 1981 formation of AV-8B 161396 and an AV-8A 159255 shows the much greater volume available in the new nose and cockpit areas. Another contrast is the lateral area of the twin under-fuselage strakes.

supersonic speed would actually make the aircraft slower. Thus, the AV-16 S-6 had a well-swept wing of low aspect ratio and very low thickness/chord ratio, with broad streamwise tips and long root extensions. High-altitude Mach number was 1.95.

With a PCB thrust of 34,500lb (15 650kg) the attractions of such a machine were obvious, and it would probably have met with the approval of the US Navy, which did not wish to bother with a mere "warmed over" version of the existing Harrier. But the likely costs were already daunting, inflation was beginning to bite, and the only really definite and urgently concerned customer, the Marine Corps, was horrified at the idea of such a complete redesign and merely wanted a more capable subsonic bomb truck. At the time it seemed tragic that, because of narrow-minded conflict of interest and perhaps also the sheer diversity of possible aircraft, the idea of a really big two-nation, four-customer programme was by 1973 falling apart.

It was especially disheartening to lose the US Navy, because in terms of numbers this was potentially the No 1 customer. On 13 October 1972 Navair, the Naval Air Systems Command, awarded a major V/STOL development contract to North American Rockwell for the extremely advanced and complex XFV-12A. This was expected to hover in August 1974 and make transitions a month later. We are still waiting for the XFV-12 to fly, and in fact the whole project fell so short of prediction it was abandoned in 1980. But its very existence could easily have caused MCAIR to look for easier lines of business, and it is to the credit of Sandy McDonnell – who inherited from his uncle a very tough and canny business sense – that instead of dropping the rejected AV-16 the St Louis company continued to believe that it was the right way to go.

To offer encouragement, in 1973 the US Marine Corps issued a formal requirement for such an Advanced Harrier, and MCAIR and Hawker began doing joint studies, which culminated in a submission to the US and British governments of an "AV-16A" on 13 December 1973. It had the MCAIR long-span supercritical wing, the Pegasus 15 engine, and numerous lift-improving detail refinements throughout the airframe. But

Left: Never has an aircraft programme of recent years started out so good on paper yet proved so great a disappointment as the US Navy Rockwell XFV-12A. Planned as a supersonic successor to the AV-8A, it never flew.

factors outside the programme were casting a deepening shadow. One was the continuing uncertainty of what the customers wanted. Only the Marines simply wanted an AV-16A. The RAF wanted an Advanced Harrier whose major improvements could be retrofitted to its existing Harriers, and on this count the MCAIR wing and Pegasus 15 engine were both non-starters. The Royal Navy had by this time become committed to the design that became the Sea Harrier. Worst of all, inflation was beginning to bite, and not only was the development cost of the AV-16A and its engine put at $1 billion but this was expected to double because of inflation by the time the aircraft entered service.

Increasingly the meetings dwelt on problems rather than progress, and what seemed to be the *coup de grâce* was the announcement of the British government on 19 March 1975 that: "There is not enough common ground on the Advanced Harrier for us to join in the programme with the US". In fact, this was not true, because one aeroplane will now serve both countries, but that particular government simply wanted to cut defence spending and was delighted to latch on to any project that seemed to be in difficulties. In the United States Navair cancelled its sponsorship of the AV-16A due to lack of funds. The Navy itself had already picked the XFV-12A, and terminating the "foreign program" pleased a lot of partisan Congressmen.

Pegasus 15 abandoned

Though this was the low point in a protracted story, the crunch in 1975 did allow each airframe partner, if it chose to, to press ahead with its own unfettered studies for its own customers. Both quickly came to the same conclusion regarding the Pegasus 15. It is possible that, had PCB development never been shelved by Rolls-Royce following cancellation of the P.1154, a 34,500lb (15650kg) PCB Pegasus 15 would have been funded in 1975, with dramatic long-term results. But the Mk 15 engine alone was costed at $600 million to US qualification, and, when it was found that this equated to $200,000 per pound of extra thrust, the whole project seemed not worth while. The crucial decision was taken to abandon any immediate major Pegasus development, and concentrate on the airframe instead. Navair funded a study of Pegasus alternatives, carried out jointly by Pratt & Whitney and Rolls-Royce, which suggested: 1, the Pegasus 104, as later adopted for the Sea Harrier; 2, the Mk 104 with internal changes to improve maintainability and give a TBO (time between overhauls) of 1,000h; 3, the Pegasus 11D with small internal changes giving 800lb (363kg) more thrust; and 4, an 11D with 1,000h TBO. Not submitted, Rolls also studied the 11D+ with increased temperature and 22,500lb (10206kg) thrust.

For a possible Advanced Harrier for the Marines, Navair picked the second choice above, the improved Mk 104 with 1,000h TBO, and with virtually all the detail improvements aimed at improving ease of maintenance and reducing total costs over perhaps a 20-year period rather than at increasing performance. Despite this, MCAIR had already shown in 1975 that by airframe modifications alone, the payload/range capability of the AV-8A could be at least *doubled*!

MCAIR were in any case determined to continue Advanced Harrier development for the Marines, and in 1975 had put a growing technical team on the job. It could have elected to go it alone, but wisely chose to continue collaboration with Hawker, who retained liaison engineers at St Louis and played a significant part in the design of what by 1975 had become the AV-8B. Before the end of 1975 MCAIR had completed the basic project design, and had already carried out extensive test programmes. One of the latter was to rebuild a crashed AV-8A to look broadly like the AV-8B, and this impressive non-flying demonstration aircraft was rolled out as early as 7 August 1975.

The obvious new feature of the AV-8B was the wing. This was a refined version of the Whitcomb supercritical wing, designed by an MCAIR team under T. R. Lacey. Its chief new feature is that, in one of the boldest structural decisions for many years, its entire primary structure is carbon-fibre composite (called graphite composite in the USA), and it is the largest carbon item in any aircraft, excepting the Rockwell B-1 horizontal tail. On any count it is larger than the Harrier wing, with span over 30ft (9·1m) and a much deeper cross-section, the average t/c (thickness to chord) ratio being 10·5 per cent compared with 8·5. Thus it can accommodate almost twice as much fuel as the original wing, 4,950lb (2245kg) compared with 2,834lb (1285kg), besides giving far greater STO lift and providing for three pylons on each side. It has eight spars, each with an undulat-

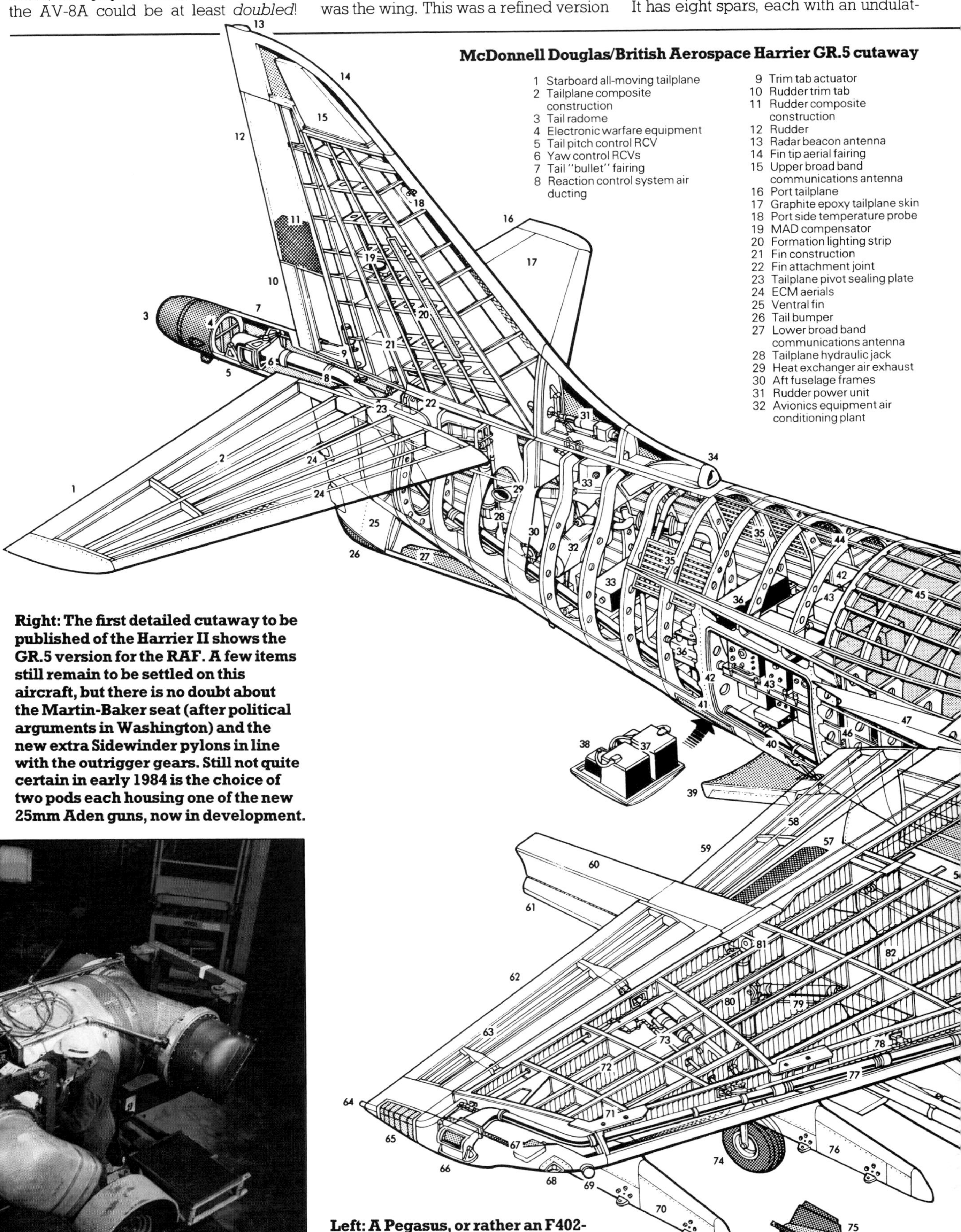

Right: The first detailed cutaway to be published of the Harrier II shows the GR.5 version for the RAF. A few items still remain to be settled on this aircraft, but there is no doubt about the Martin-Baker seat (after political arguments in Washington) and the new extra Sidewinder pylons in line with the outrigger gears. Still not quite certain in early 1984 is the choice of two pods each housing one of the new 25mm Aden guns, now in development.

Left: A Pegasus, or rather an F402-404A, for a Full-Scale Development AV-8B is checked over before its first bench run at Rolls-Royce Bristol. Externally the chief new feature is the long zero-scarf front nozzle. The heavy blue plate around it is test gear.

AV-8B structural materials

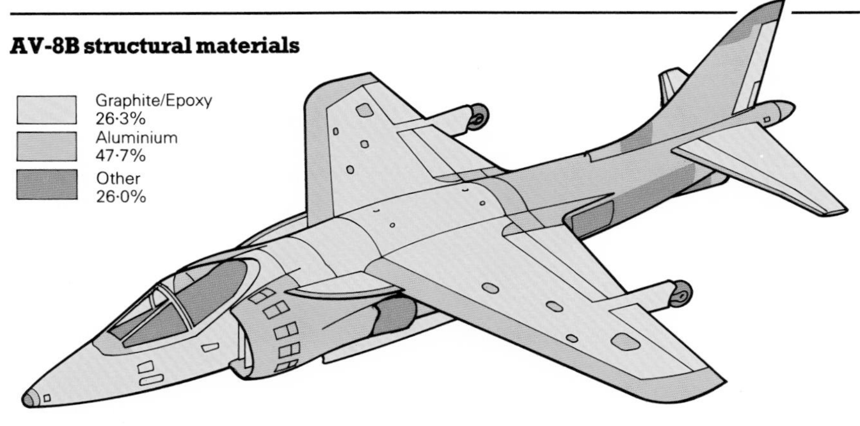

Above: Another far from obvious new feature of all Harrier II aircraft is the widespread use of graphite composite.

The 26·3 per cent by weight equates to about 40 per cent by volume, because of the low density of this material.

ing (sine-wave) web, yet the switch to carbon and deeper profile enables the new wing to weigh 330lb (150kg) less than an equivlent all-metal wing.

The leading edge is now swept at 36° instead of 40°, and is a simple aluminium alloy structure which after flight development has only a single outboard fence. The trailing edge is totally new. While the RCVs are right at the tip, for maximum roll power, the outrigger landing gears have been moved inboard between the ailerons and flaps, reducing track to 17ft (5·18m) for easier manoeuvring and with the leg fairings replaced by doors. Inboard are the enormous double-slotted flaps which in the STO mode are extended to 62° and react powerfully with the wing circulation induced by the angled nozzles. MCAIR and NASA conducted prolonged tests to rearrange the nozzles, wing and flaps to obtain the most favourable circulation around the inboard wing in STO. This work also led to new longer zero-scarf front engine nozzles which give 200lb (91kg) more thrust. It is planned to switch to titanium, saving 50lb (22·7kg). This wing/flap/nozzle improvement provides the largest of the many increments in STO lift, no less than 6,700lb (3039kg) on a 1,000ft (300m) run.

The new engine inlets were further refined to increase airflow and reduce drag, and the geometry of the double row of auxiliary inlet doors improved. Eventually, at the seventeenth production AV-8B, it was found possible to use large single doors. These increase VTO lift by 600lb (272kg), but instead of this

33 Avionics equipment racks
34 Heat exchanger ram air intake
35 Electrical system circuit breaker panels, port and starboard
36 Electronic warfare equipment
37 Chaff and flare dispensers
38 Dispenser electronic control units
39 Ventral airbrake
40 Airbrake hydraulic jack
41 Formation lighting strip
42 Avionics bay access door, port and starboard
43 Avionics equipment racks
44 Fuselage frame and stringer construction
45 Rear fuselage fuel tank
46 Main undercarriage wheel bay
47 Wing root fillet
48 Wing spar/fuselage attachment joint
49 Water filler cap
50 Engine fire extinguisher bottle
51 Anti-collision light
52 Water tank
53 Flap power unit
54 Flap hinge fitting
55 Titanium fuselage heat shield
56 Main undercarriage bay doors (closed after cycling of mainwheels)
57 Flap vane composite construction
58 Flap composite construction
59 Starboard slotted flap, lowered
60 Outrigger wheel fairing
61 Outrigger leg doors
62 Starboard aileron
63 Aileron composite construction
64 Fuel jettison
65 Formation lighting panel
66 Roll control RCV
67 Radar warning signal processor
68 Starboard navigation light
69 Radar warning aerial
70 Outboard pylon
71 Pylon attachment joint
72 Graphite epoxy composite wing construction
73 Aileron power unit
74 Starboard outrigger wheel
75 BL755 600lb (272kg) cluster bomb (CBU)
76 Intermediate pylon
77 Reaction control air ducting
78 Aileron control rod
79 Outrigger hydraulic retraction jack
80 Outrigger leg strut
81 Leg pivot fixing
82 Multi-spar graphite wing construction
83 Leading-edge wing fence
84 Outrigger pylon
85 Missile launch rail
86 AIM-9L Sidewinder air-to-air missile
87 External fuel tank, 300US Gal (1135lit)
88 Inboard pylon
89 Aft retracting twin mainwheels
90 Inboard pylon attachment joint
91 Rear (hot stream) swivelling exhaust nozzle
92 Position of pressure refuelling connection on port side
93 Rear nozzle bearing
94 Centre fuselage flank tank
95 Hydraulic reservoir
96 Nozzle bearing cooling air duct
97 Engine exhaust divider duct
98 Wing panel centre rib
99 Centre section integral fuel tank
100 Port wing integral fuel tank
101 Flap vane
102 Port slotted flap, lowered
103 Outrigger wheel fairing
104 Port outrigger wheel
105 Torque scissor links
106 Port aileron
107 Aileron power unit
108 Aileron/air valve interconnection
109 Fuel jettison
110 Formation lighting panel
111 Port roll control RCV
112 Port navigation light
113 Radar warning aerial
114 Port wing reaction control air duct
115 Fuel pumps
116 Fuel system piping
117 Port wing leading-edge fence
118 Outboard pylon
119 BL755 cluster bombs (maximum load, seven)
120 Intermediate pylon
121 Port outrigger pylon
122 Missile launch rail
123 AIM-9L Sidewinder air-to-air missile
124 Port leading-edge root extension (LERX)
125 Inboard pylon
126 Hydraulic pumps
127 APU intake
128 Gas turbine starter/auxiliary power unit (APU)
129 Alternator cooling air exhaust
130 APU exhaust
131 Engine fuel control unit
132 Engine bay venting ram air intake
133 Rotary nozzle bearing
134 Nozzle fairing construction
135 Ammunition tank, 110 rounds
136 Cartridge case collector box
137 Ammunition feed chute
138 Fuel vent
139 Gun pack strake
140 Fuselage centreline pylon
141 Zero scarf forward (fan air) nozzle
142 Ventral gun pack (two)
143 Aden 25mm cannon
144 Engine drain mast
145 Hydraulic system ground connectors
146 Forward fuselage flank fuel tank
147 Engine electronic control units
148 Engine accessory equipment gearbox
149 Gearbox driven alternator
150 Rolls-Royce Pegasus 11 Mk 105 vectored thrust turbofan
151 Formation lighting strips
152 Engine oil tank
153 Bleed air spill duct
154 Air conditioning intake scoops
155 Cockpit air conditioning system heat exchanger
156 Engine compressor/fan face
157 Heat exchanger discharge to intake duct
158 Nose undercarriage hydraulic retraction jack
159 Intake blow-in doors
160 Engine bay venting air scoop
161 Cannon muzzle fairing
162 Lift augmentation retractable cross-dam
163 Cross-dam hydraulic jack
164 Nosewheel
165 Nosewheel forks
166 Landing/taxiing lamp
167 Retractable boarding step
168 Nosewheel doors (closed after cycling of undercarriage)
169 Nosewheel door jack
170 Boundary layer bleed air duct
171 Nose undercarriage wheel bay
172 Kick-in boarding steps
173 Cockpit rear pressure bulkhead
174 Starboard side console panel
175 Martin-Baker Mk 10 ejection seat
176 Safety harness
177 Ejection seat headrest
178 Port engine air intake
179 Probe hydraulic jack
180 Retractable inflight-refuelling probe (bolt-on pack)
181 Cockpit canopy cover
182 Miniature detonating cord (MDC) canopy breaker
183 Canopy frame
184 Engine throttle and nozzle control levers
185 Pilot's head-up-display (HUD)
186 Instrument panel
187 Moving map display
188 Control column
189 Central warning system panel
190 Cockpit pressure floor
191 Underfloor control runs
192 Formation lighting strips
193 Aileron trim actuator
194 Rudder pedals
195 Cockpit section composite construction
196 Instrument panel shroud
197 One-piece wrap-around windscreen panel
198 Ram air intake (cockpit fresh air)
199 Front pressure bulkhead
200 Incidence vane
201 Air data computer
202 Pitot tube
203 Lower IFF aerial
204 Nose pitch control air valve
205 Pitch trim control actuator
206 Electrical system equipment
207 Yaw vane
208 Upper IFF aerial
209 Electronic warfare equipment
210 ARBS heat exchanger
211 MIRLS sensors
212 Hughes Angle Rate Bombing System (ARBS)
213 Composite construction nose cone
214 ARBS glazed aperture

being at the cost of poorer high-speed behaviour the drag in cruising flight is actually reduced. Another very large contribution (1,200lb, 544kg) to VTO lift is furnished by the greatly improved LIDs (lift-improvement devices), which were devised jointly by BAe and MCAIR. Even the mid-1975 AV-8B mock-up had strakes added to the gun pods, with the inter-pod space boxed in by a hinged surface upstream – called a dam, but looking like an airbrake – which when tested on an AV-8A not only increased low-altitude lift by 1,220lb (533kg) but also reduced hot-gas reingestion and lowered inlet temperature by 20°C.

As well as being modified in shape, the complete forward fuselage, horizontal tail, rudder and the removable panels covering the top of the fuselage were all redesigned in carbon fibre. An incidental advantage is the elimination of tailplane resonance problems, and this is hoped to extend also to the proposed TAV-8B two-seater. As for the cockpit, this has been raised 10·5in (267mm) and provided with a giant circular-profile canopy giving an outstanding all-round view. The cockpit is descibed later. The whole nose was greatly enlarged, to provide additional space for avionics and other equipment, and the front windshield was increased in size and made a single curved piece of very thick multilayer stretched acrylic, with deicing but no wiper.

These were the chief improvements proposed by MCAIR for the AV-8B, which continued at full pressure at St Louis, assisted by NASA, though not yet funded by the Navy. By early 1976 another damaged AV-8A had been rebuilt with many AV-8B features, including the wing, flaps, LIDs and engine inlets, and initially put through engine-running and lift interaction tests resting on tall supports out of doors. By September 1976 it was in the giant 40×80ft tunnel at NASA's Ames Research Center. This full-scale model, whose wing was made of aluminium and wood, completed 319h of testing, and smaller models completed over 4,000h in perfecting the new high-lift features of the AV-8B.

Above: The third FSD aircraft, seen here near St Louis in April 1982, was the first to be fitted with LERX at the wing roots. This photograph illustrates the excellent visibility from the cockpit; the pilot is head up during air-to-air and air-to-ground combat.

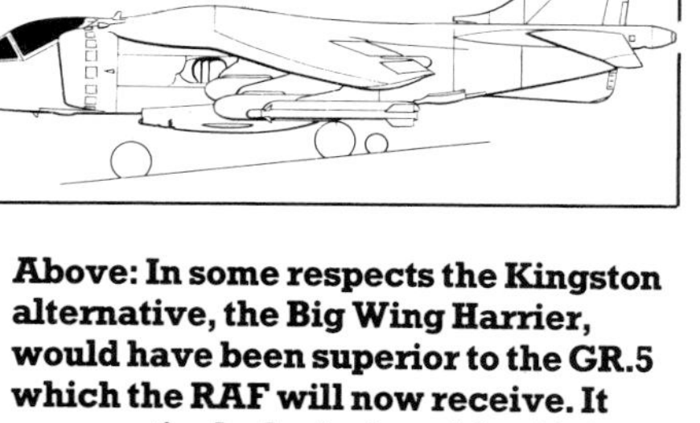

Above: In some respects the Kingston alternative, the Big Wing Harrier, would have been superior to the GR.5 which the RAF will now receive. It was particularly designed for higher speed and better manoeuvrability.

Below: Aerodynamicists festoon prototype aircraft with tufts to explore airflow and look for flow breakaway. Here a YAV-8B, 158394, has tufting covering the entire top and bottom of both wings. Inboard stores are Snakeye bombs.

Funding is authorized

In March 1976 William P. Clements Jr, the US Deputy Secretary for Defense, announced agreement in principle to a programme for 342 AV-8B aircraft for the Marine Corps, comprising two YAV-8B prototypes, four FSD (full-scale development) prototypes and 336 production machines. Later the 336 were to be divided into 12 pilot production, 18 limited production and 306 full production. Limited funding was authorized, including cover for the two prototypes, and a complete test example of the new wing. To save time and cost the two YAV-8Bs were rebuilt AV-8As, Nos 158394 and 158395. These incorporated the complete new wing, with carbon (graphite) structure, but not yet incorporating production-style manufacturing methods, as well as the new inlets, and LIDs, but retaining the original tailplane, forward fuselage, cockpit and internal systems. The first YAV was completed 53 days ahead of schedule and at 188lb (85·3kg) under the calculated empty weight, so that it weighed almost exactly the same as a regular Harrier. AV-8B Project Test Pilot Charley Plummer lifted off from the concrete apron at Lambert St Louis airport for the first time on 9 November 1978.

In March 1979 ski takeoffs began from the Fairey-built MGB 12° ramp which had been purchased by the US Navy and airlifted from Farnborough to Pax River. A month later, in April 1979, MCAIR was awarded the long-awaited contract for the four FSD aircraft, and a long-lead contract for $35 million to begin preparation for production. At the same time it was by this time all too evident that the AV-8B was still tainted with the hated label "foreign" in influential sections of Congress. Though it had no historical precedent, the Carter administration decided to put the screws on the RAF to buy the AV-8B rather than the home-grown Big-Wing Harrier by making a full go-ahead on the AV-8B contingent upon export sales. Many partisan things were said, and certainly there existed a powerful lobby who wanted all the Navy vote to be poured into the colossal and escalating funding-trough of the F/A-18A Hornet (from the same contractor) and major ship programmes. SecDef Harold S. Brown called the F/A-18A-only choice a "more efficient" solution, overlooking the fact that a distant Marines beach-head might offer no conventional air-base. Another DoD spokesman called the AV-8B "an inefficient project that consumes funds needed for overall force modernization".

Probably the most serious result of the three years of delaying tactics for political ends was an increase in the estimated US price for the programme of no less than £920 million, due solely to infla-

Above: BuAer No 158394, the first YAV-8B, caught by the camera in a tight turn over the Patuxent River runways in early 1982. Note the two cine cameras under the rear fuselage, aft of the old Aden-shape gun pods.

tion. Had the RAF simply bought the AV-8B at the start there might have been no delay at all, but the British situation was not easy to resolve. The RAF's needs continued to be for an improved Harrier able not only to fly far and fast at the lowest possible level, in the face of bad weather and intense hostile electronics and ordnance, but also to dogfight when necessary against agile opponents. Air Staff Requirement 409 stipulated various numerical parameters, including a maximum speed not less than that of the GR.3 and a sustained turn-rate of 20°/s. Hawker (BAe from 1978) strove to meet all the RAF's needs, and also to do so with changes which could be retroactively applied to existing RAF Harriers. It succeeded on all counts, with its proposed Big-Wing Harrier, produced to MoD study contract in 1978-80 and noteworthy for a fully swept long-span (over 34ft) wing made in metal and not only retrofittable but also with a high-speed profile for low drag and high manoeuvrability. Prominent at the roots of the leading edge were LERX (leading-edge root extensions) to add area at high AOA and create strong vortices, and thus delay the onset of flow separation from above the wing. They have a deliberate destabilizing effect and, seen in various forms on most modern air-combat aircraft, they enhance manoeuvrability. Tested on a GR.3 (XV277) they enabled pilots to pull 1g extra at any given engine thrust.

The Big Wing Harrier proposed many other new features, and would have had no fewer than ten stores attachments on the wings alone. BAe thought it at least as saleable as the AV-8B, which was slower than the GR.3 and missed meeting the RAF turn rate by miles with a limit of under 14°/s. It therefore produced brochures to try to convince governments, notably the British, that it had the better product and that it would be better for Britain to have the whole of an initially modest RAF programme, with a big export potential, than a minor share of the AV-8B. The decision was agonizing, but the carpet was rather pulled from under BAe when the Minister of Defence announced in 1980 that "the Big Wing is unlikely to be any part of an improvement programme for the GR.3". Though deadlock appeared to continue, in fact BAe very reluctantly came round to the view that half a cake is better than the whole of a non-starter, and in January 1981, as the new Reagan administration took office in Washington, BAe recommended acceptance of the AV-8B as the most commercially viable solution.

At last the Minister of Defence announced in July 1981 that the AV-8B would be bought for the RAF, with an expected total of 60 aircraft. Much fewer than the original Harrier buy, this will equip new squadrons to serve alongside GR.3 units, the latter aircraft being given a major mid-life update. At once there was what previous SecDef Brown had

Below: AV-8B No 5, the first true production Harrier II, in the St Louis plant with F-15s in the rear in April 1983. Note the double row of inlet doors, which have now been replaced by single doors of improved form.

Above: The "pretty" FSD aircraft, 161397, on test from St Louis in April 1982 with gear extended and a touch of airbrake. LERX and LIDs are installed.

called "a new situation", and an MOU (Memorandum of Understanding) was signed on 24 August 1981 authorizing full-scale development. MCAIR and BAe decided on the family name Harrier II. The deal at the industrial level finally thrashed out is: for all US and 75 per cent of third-country sales, MCAIR is prime contractor with BAe a subcontractor; for all UK and 25 per cent of third-country sales, BAe is prime, with MCAIR a subcontractor; actual split of airframe work is about 60 MCAIR to 40 BAe; and systems and equipment are split about 80 US to 20 UK. The engine is a far better deal for Rolls-Royce, which merely has to relinquish up to 25 per cent of the production content to Pratt & Whitney, and for the Marine Corps buy only.

One advantage of the delay in launching full-scale development was that it was possible to crank in numerous further updates to both the aircraft and engine. The latter progressed from the YF402-RR-404, used in the YAV-8B aircraft, to the F402-404 with an improved 1st fan stage with wide-root blades to permit higher rpm, a higher-output gearbox and a new bulkhead matched to the production AV-8B. This was cleared at 21,700lb (9843kg) in 1980, and in the same year running began on a further improved sub-variant, the Dash-404A, with a revised swan-neck (intermediate casing) with a more efficient air path, and an increased-capacity No 2 bearing. In the same year, 1980, testing began of the full production engine, the F402-RR-406, with the shrouded LP turbine, triple interstage labyrinth seals, improved HP turbine cooling and a forged combustion-chamber outlet. Rated at 22,000lb (9979kg), this promises to be cleared to 1,000h TBO, with a hot-end inspection at 500h. In RAF service it will be designated Pegasus 105. The Dash-406 will enter service with the Marines in 1985, replacing the Dash-404A now being used in AV-8Bs.

The advantage of composites

The first of the four FSD aircraft flew in Plummer's hands at St Louis on 5 November 1981. All four were flying by June 1982, and two further airframes were built for structural testing, a novel feature of the AV-8B being that as no fatigue is yet known in carbon composite structures the wing and tailplane should have unlimited life. By July 1982 the fatigue specimen had completed 24,000h, equal to two planned lifetimes each of 12,000 flying hours. Further work led to the introduction of improved structural manufacturing and test methods, such as accurately cutting out large numbers of stacked carbon composite plies (laminates) simultaneously, and automatically traversing an ultrasonic scanner over the entire wing skins to check on perfect inter-laminate bonding.

More fundamental have been the improvements to the on-board systems. Nobody was ever totally satisfied with the original Harrier stability and control which in one band of airspeeds during a transition could lead via a yaw and involuntary roll to complete loss of control The Harrier II has a new high-authority SAAHS (stability and attitude-hold system) with a pitch/roll autostabilization computer and an electronic interface to the front RCV. Longitudinal and lateral margins are greatly improved, and with SAAHS operative throughout the flight envelope the pilot workload is greatly reduced, and anxiety virtually eliminated. Writing in *Rolls-Royce Magazine* the AV-8B Program Manager at Pax River, Maj Richard H. Priest, commented "It sounds good, but how does that translate when I'm trying to land on a 72ft by 72ft pad in the trees, or on a pitching deck on a dark night? I lower the nozzles and begin deceleration. I quickly realise that almost no lateral stick inputs are required, and the classic AV-8A nose wander is just not there any more. Continuing the decel to hover I am again impressed by the rock-steady feel of the aircraft, and how cool the engine is running under these demanding conditions.

AV-8B avionics aerials (antennas)

This diagram shows the locations of the main avionics aerials of the Marines' AV-8B. Many, but not all, will be common to the RAF Harrier GR.5.

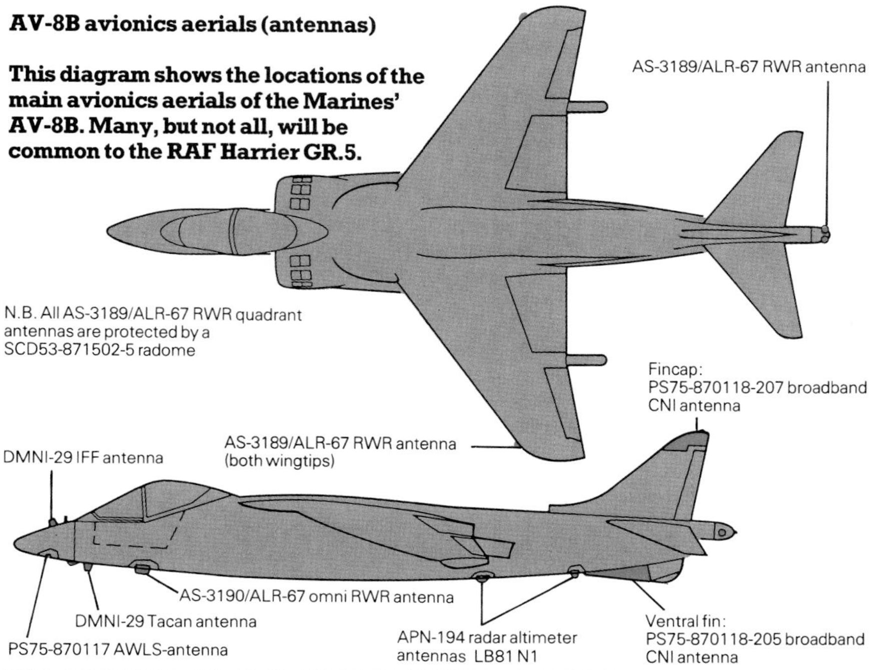

AS-3189/ALR-67 RWR antenna

N.B. All AS-3189/ALR-67 RWR quadrant antennas are protected by a SCD53-871502-5 radome

Fincap: PS75-870118-207 broadband CNI antenna

AS-3189/ALR-67 RWR antenna (both wingtips)

DMNI-29 IFF antenna

AS-3190/ALR-67 omni RWR antenna

DMNI-29 Tacan antenna

PS75-870117 AWLS-antenna

APN-194 radar altimeter antennas LB81 N1

Ventral fin: PS75-870118-205 broadband CNI antenna

Reducing the power to descend to about 15ft I wait for the cobblestoning [random attitude disturbances] to begin, but it never occurs." In fact, so effective are the LIDs that AV-8B pilots just let the aircraft mush down on to the air cushion, where it refuses to sink any further until the power is brought back.

In production AV-8Bs propulsion management is handled by a Fadec (full-authority digital electronic control) produced by the new group DSIC (Dowty and Smiths Industries Controls). The AV-8B is the first production application for a Fadec, which again reduces pilot workload and any peaks in turbine gas temperature. As part of a far-ranging five-year NASA research programme into AV-8B stability and vectored-thrust aircraft behaviour generally, which will spin-off into future fighter designs, it is planned in late 1984 to integrate the throttle and nozzle controls into a single cockpit control, so that the pilot can fly in true Hotas (hands on throttle and stick) style, without ever having to move his left hand from one control to another. This will give perfect Viffing control for air combat, in which the AV-8B is already proving formidable, and will also ease the pilot's task in bad weather landings and other challenging phases of flight.

The NASA study has further tasks, including the refinement of simulator models to develop new navigation and guidance concepts for use in bad weather, including essentially blind landings impossible with other combat aircraft.

System improvements

Typical of system improvements throughout the aircraft, the Harrier II flap control system is digital FBW (fly by wire). It is self-monitoring, and controls the two electrohydraulic power units, each of which can push with 30,000lb (13·6 tonnes) to move the flaps at 7°/s down to 25° and at 64°/s from 25° to 62°. In earlier Harriers breakage of the torque tubes linking the flaps could cause flap asymmetry and force the pilot to eject. With the Harrier II the flap system can suffer any kind of failure and even shut down, yet the pilot can still fly the aircraft. The system also controls droop of the two ailerons, which improves lift in STO or at high AOA, and eliminates the need for the pilot to adjust flap setting in flight. Other major system improvements include constant-frequency AC electrics, an updated inertial navigation system (ASN-130 in the AV-8B, possibly a different system for the GR.5) and an Obogs (on-board oxygen generating system) which passes engine bleed air through filter beds which remove everything but the oxygen, as it is needed.

Left: The original planning cockpit used in defining the standard for the Harrier GR.5. The head-down moving-map display is on the right, and the MFD on the left is shown in the stores readout mode.

Below left: An early AV-8B simulator (July 1979), though with a cockpit not very different from those in today's production aircraft. Here the RAF moving-map display is replaced by the panels for fuel and ALE-39 ECM.

It goes without saying that the Harrier II cockpit is totally new. A great deal was fed in from the F/A-18A programme, including a large MFD (multifunction display) on the left and a prominent and easily used UFC (up-front control) for CNI (com/nav/ident) which incorporates a fibre-optic data converter. Above the UFC is the large Smiths Industries HUD, with dual combiner glasses, and on the right is a fuel panel and another controlling the Goodyear ALE-39 chaff/flare dispenser in the rear fuselage (in the GR.5 the RAF plan to have a moving-map display here instead). The armament control panel is low on the left, below the MFD.

At present all Harrier IIs have an approximately similar Hotas system, the stick and throttle grips including the following control functions: SAAHS control, air start, manoeuvre flaps (for combat), com selection, sensor selection, sensor cage/uncage, slew control/designation, weapon selection, weapon release, gun firing and aircraft trim. Viffing for combat will later be added to this impressive list. Pilot view is superb, and unlike the original low-canopied Harrier the pilot can sit well upright yet still find that the HUD is dead centre in his forward FOV (field of view). Previously, pilots sat as high as possible to try to see out, and then could not get down to use the HUD; "Harrier hunch" became famous throughout the Marine Corps. With the second-generation aircraft there is no need to hunch, and all controls also are comfortably situated without need to move the body.

Above: This drawing depicts an RAF Harrier GR.5. Stores shown include GP bombs, BL.755 CBUs and Lepus flares. LIDs strakes are fitted, though the expected gun pod is the new 25mm Aden. The RWR installation is the same ALR-67 as used by the US Marine Corps, with forward-facing aerials on the wingtips, though a different RWR may be selected.

There would be little problem in accommodating a modern multimode radar, but in all Harrier IIs at present planned the primary weapon delivery sensor is the Hughes ARBS (angle rate bombing system). This is mounted in the extreme nose and comprises a laser spot tracker and TV contrast tracker working together. They can be locked on to any surface target and thereafter continuously feed the appropriate angle rate information to the HUD and, if it is set in the attack mode, the MFD. The laser receiver also detects and locks on to any target illuminated by a correctly coded friendly laser from elsewhere. The pilot need make only one pass, and can lay down iron bombs manually, or by computer-controlled AWR (auto weapons release) mode, or by the CCIP (continuously computed impact point) line or depressed-sightline modes. Alternatively he can select missiles, such as any variant of Maverick or LGBs (laser-guided bombs).

Harrier GR.5s will probably stick to the Aden (though presumably in a 25mm developed version), but the AV-8B is the first aircraft to use the American General Electric GAU-12/U. This is the newest of the GE "Gatling" family, and has five barrels of 25mm (0.984in) calibre. MCAIR and GE developed a unique armament system in which the gun is mounted in the left-hand pod and 300 rounds of ammunition are housed in the right pod, which is aerodynamically identical. Behind the gun is the 35hp pneumatic drive motor running on engine bleed air. Rate of fire is 3,600spm (thrice the 30mm Aden rate) and muzzle velocity is 1,065m/s compared with 790. The magazine is very easy to reload, and with a linkless feed nothing is left behind on board. As previously noted, the pods have been configured to enhance the air-cushion effect as part of the LIDs programme. Other ordnance and external loads are listed in a diagram. The maximum weapon carriage of 9,200lb (4173kg) has been demonstrated.

Below: An assortment of wing-mounted or centreline stores (not the gun pods) carried during Navy Board of Inspection and Survey trials. In front are a Sidewinder training store, an AIM-9L and a pair of AIM-9Ns.

In-flight refuelling

MCAIR test pilot Jack Jackson flew the first of the 12 pilot-production AV-8Bs in a 1h shakedown from Lambert St Louis on 29 August 1983. The general feeling at St Louis is that each Harrier II is coming out better than its predecessors, but with the pilot-production machines the definitive standard is very closely approached. A few weeks previously Jackson had made the first wet hookup with a Marine KC-130 tanker operating from Edwards. The neat refuelling probe, which is removable, retracts into the top of the left inlet duct fairing and when extended is easily visible to the pilot. Despite what Jackson knew from experience was severe turbulence behind the tanker, which often causes other aircraft to make an inadvertent disconnect, the AV-8B was rock-steady. Jackson said his workload was "about half that needed with an AV-8A".

Later, in late November 1983, the Navy reached final agreement on several important procurements in FY83 and FY84. The total obligational funding (paying for everything) for the AV-8B for these two fiscal years was planned to be 18 in FY83 costed at $942·9 million and 30 in FY84 at $979·8 million. The actual contractual figure for the basic aircraft (minus engine) for FY83 had been set at $423·6 million, for an increased buy of 21 aircraft, but this has been further pruned to $401·3 million. Delivery of pilot-production aircraft to the Marine Corps began in October 1983, and, as this book went to press, production was gradually building up to the planned 4·5 aircraft per month. The pilot-production aircraft are followed by the 18 so-called limited-production AV-8Bs, beyond which come the 306 full-production aircraft.

It is planned that by late 1988 the Marines should have 260 of these aircraft, with IOC (initial operational capa-

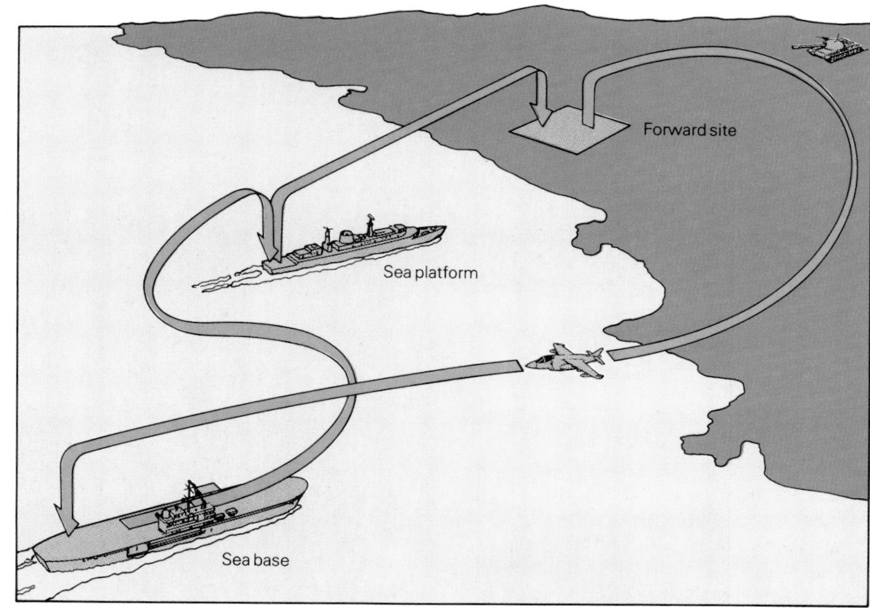

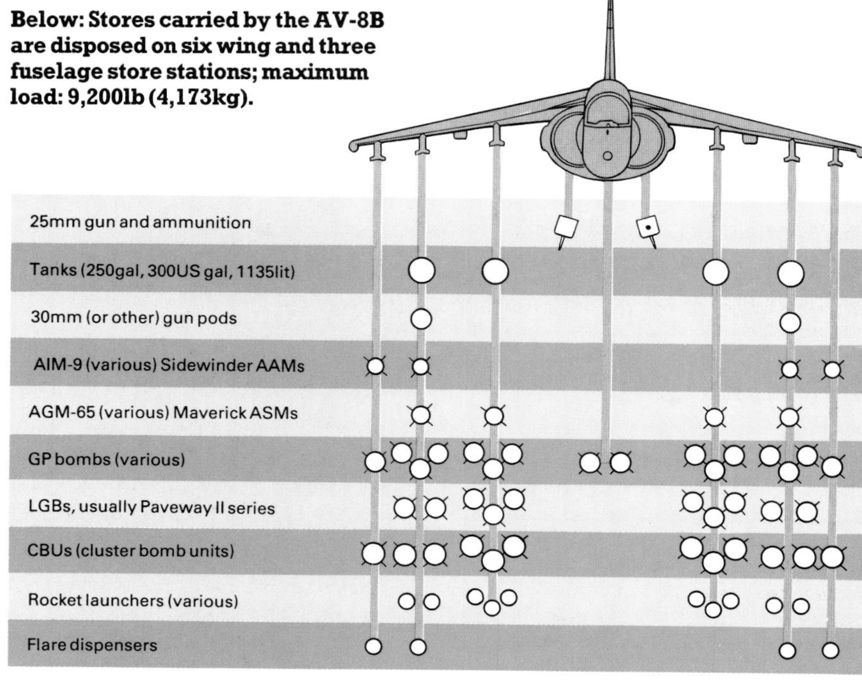

Below: Stores carried by the AV-8B are disposed on six wing and three fuselage store stations; maximum load: 9,200lb (4,173kg).

Harrier II mission profiles

Left: Simplified mission diagram showing AV-8B operation from sea bases against land targets. The very flexible Harrier family could do a VTO or, as shown on a *Tarawa* class ship, an STO. A brief visit is made to the helicopter pad of a surface warship, followed by a VL at a forward site on land, before returning to the original ship.

Right: Here a selection of possible AV-8B shore-based missions is shown. A rolling takeoff would usually be made wherever possible, and certainly at the main base (unless rendered totally unusable). The forward sites would if possible be camouflaged, and most would probably offer only a very restricted run. Tanks imply hostile ground forces.

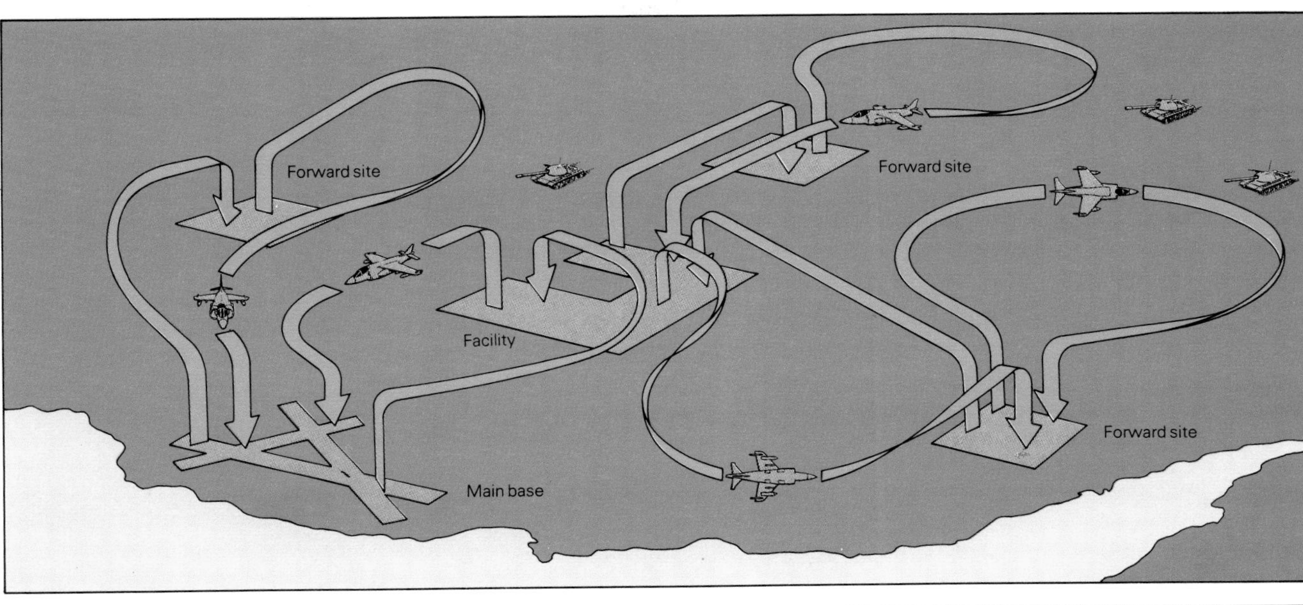

bility) achieved from mid-1985. Initially the Harrier IIs will replace the AV-8C in VMAT-203, VMA-231 and VMA-542, the surviving older Harriers going to reserve units. Further Harrier IIs will then replace the A-4 Skyhawk in the five Marine squadrons still flying this aircraft. To support the pilot training requirement, especially in conversion of the A-4 pilots, it is planned to purchase 18 two-seat TAV-8Bs. These are likely to differ substantially from the British two-seater even in the changes compared with the single-seat version. Length would be increased by 4ft (1·22m) and tail height by 17in (432mm), both close to the British figures, but the AV-8B starting point has a totally new forward fuselage and the trainer will have a shorter tailcone. The front (pupil) cockpit would omit the ECM systems and, initially, weapon-delivery controls, though the TAV-8B would be designed to be used if necessary as a combat aircraft.

With the Harrier II now firmly established as a production aircraft it must be expected that it will become the standard international version. British Aerospace are only too aware of the possibilities, and may be expected, in partnership with MCAIR, to offer a naval shipboard variant in due course. Meanwhile the first export order, for 12, was announced by the Spanish Navy in April 1983. These aircraft will be very close to the Marine Corps AV-8B, though they may be delivered with the 11-21 engine. The contract is priced at $378 million, with spares and training included. From early 1987 these aircraft will equip the new squadron to be based aboard the *Príncipe de Asturias*, the new Spanish V/STOL carrier. The VA-1 Matadors will continue in service with Esc 008, unlike the early Harriers of the US Marine Corps. The Spanish AV-8B squadron has not yet been announced.

Above: A September 1983 photograph of a production AV-8B showing the ARBS in the nose and the GE 25mm gun and ammunition pod installation. The only change since then has been a further improvement in the inlets.

Below: Dry and later wet contacts were made with FSD aircraft 161397 in March and April 1983, the KC-130R coming from VMGR-352. Unlike all previous Harriers the AV-8B has a retractable inflight-refuelling probe.

Below: Weapon release trials from Patuxent River in October 1982, using the third aircraft, included this set of two triplets of inert Snakeye retarded bombs. Delivery accuracy has been consistently excellent.

The Future

The regrettably limited acceptance so far of the Harrier, especially in its air force versions, is a damning indictment of air staffs who believe in the sanctity of airfields. British Aerospace and MCAIR know the penny will eventually drop, and are busy with new ways of using Harriers and with higher-performance derived designs. As the conflict in the South Atlantic revealed, the very newness of going to war with vectored thrust means that we are as yet only on the brink of the possibilities. SCADS, Skyhook, PCB: these are some of the concepts that may come to fruition during this decade.

Above: Some people might get the idea McDonnell Douglas was trying to corner the market in advanced combat aircraft. The chief point that emerges from this June 1982 formation picture is the relatively small size of the Harrier II, compared with the F-15 (nearest) and F/A-18 (furthest).

In October 1981, just before roll-out of the first AV-8B, the MCAIR AV-8B engineering director, Larry Smith, was interviewed in the following terms:

Q. In the grand scheme of things, how important is the AV-8B?

A. It's extremely important, even historic. The move to V/STOL tactical aircraft is of comparable importance to the move from propeller to jet aircraft, and I believe history will record it that way.

Q. What makes this evolution historic?

A. It's a combination not possible earlier in the history of flight, a marriage of the advantages of the fixed-wing aircraft with the advantages of the rotary-wing aircraft. If the development of those two types was historic, and it was, then the advent of fixed-wing jet V/STOL is of equal significance.

These facts are all so basic and familiar that they are easily overlooked. This is especially the case in peacetime, when the superb airbases still exist. It is only after the airbases have been blasted – even if only conventional weapons are used – that vectored thrust takes over as the only survivable form of airpower. But in many parts of the world the costly and immovable airfields have never even existed, or perhaps the only ones available belong to the enemy. Harriers can still thunder into action, in every kind of tactical role, operating from jungle clearings, highways, warship pads, merchant vessels, or anything else offering about 75ft (23m) of clear space.

Below: Today's GR.3? Sure, but what other aeroplane – anywhere in the world – can deploy real airpower without needing any kind of airfield or carrier? This aircraft from 233 OCU demonstrates the aerodynamics – using rainwater – of a rolling VL.

Of course, it helps greatly if a ski jump is available. Nobody appreciates this better than the current users of the Harrier, and it would be strange if they had not years ago have completed detailed surveys of all the many thousands of sites around the world where their V/STOLs might suddenly have to go into action from a natural ski ramp formed by the terrain. Even in desert regions it is possible to find dispersed sites offering natural ski ramps, though sandy deserts pose ingestion problems and generally make concealment difficult. Alternatively, it is possible to drive around with one's own airfield, but the early ideas for mobile ramps are now regarded as too costly.

However, there is no reason to doubt that a much simpler so-called skeletal ramp could make the task of erecting, folding, transporting and re-erecting much easier. British Aerospace proposed such a ramp in 1979. The key feature is a central rail with a deep channel section tailored to the twin-wheel main landing gear. All the pilot need do is set up the nozzle stop and bang the throttle open. The aircraft will be steered precisely and automatically, so that all the outrigger gears need are two narrow rails, possibly only 1ft (0·3m) wide. The 1979 display model showed only two support trusses, each fitted with

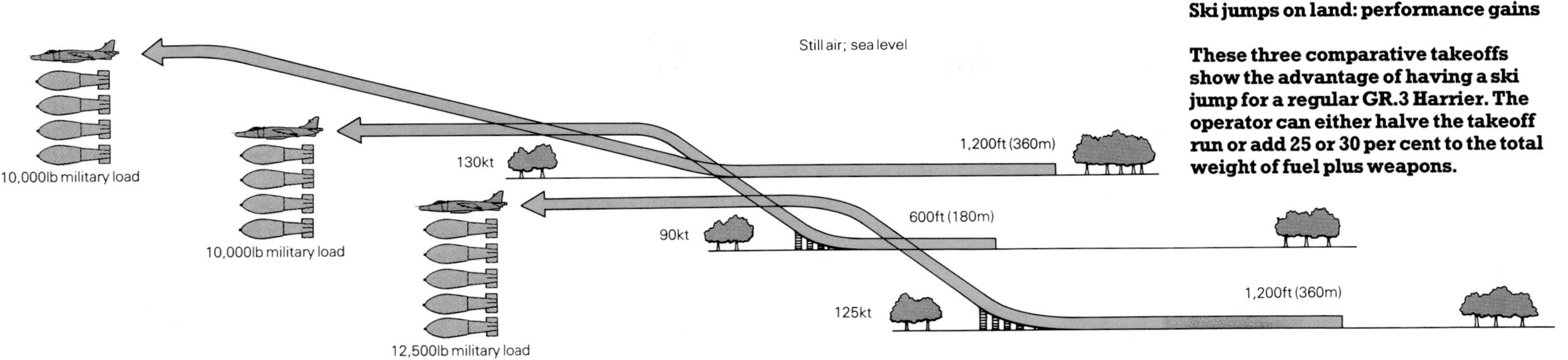

Ski jumps on land: performance gains

These three comparative takeoffs show the advantage of having a ski jump for a regular GR.3 Harrier. The operator can either halve the takeoff run or add 25 or 30 per cent to the total weight of fuel plus weapons.

Right: G-VTOL, the company demonstrator, has been used for hundreds of ski-jump takeoffs to show potential customers there really is nothing to it. Here it is using the RAE Bedford ramp which is set at 20°. The development of mobile, land-based ramps must be a priority for the future.

transport wheels but anchored to the ground prior to aircraft operations. Such a ramp would weigh approximately one-tenth as much as the MGB plate type of ski ramp, and several could be airlifted in a single C-130.

Incidentally, as more and more nations realize that a mobile ski ramp is less vulnerable than an airfield, the supply of ramps for both combat operations and training will become important. It started when in 1979 the US Marines bought the Farnborough ramp and set it up at NAS Pax River, moving it to MCAS Cherry Point as a routine training facility in 1981. They bought a second MGB ramp for the US West Coast, and are buying the kit for a ramp for their Mobile Reserve. The first permanent training ramp was designed by BAe for the Royal Navy at Yeovilton, and is unique in several respects. Its first 100ft (30m) is concrete, but the final portion can easily be adjusted in 1° intervals to any setting between 7° and 15°, which enables the ramp to duplicate those of *Invincible/Illustrious* at 7° and *Hermes/Ark Royal* at 12°.

In the maritime context the possibilities for Harrier deployment are open-ended. Consider the case of Sub-Lt Ian Watson, who ran out of fuel over the Atlantic, far from land, in June 1983. He merely alighted on a small (2,300ton) Spanish merchant ship, an operation which Watson had neither trained for nor even considered, saving a £7 million aircraft which, without vectored thrust, would have sunk. But when operations from merchant ships are premeditated, the results can be impressive. Two fascinating proposals, with possibilities which grow each time they are studied, are Skyhook and SCADS.

SCADS: a force multiplier

SCADS (shipborne containerized air-defence system) is unique in warfare. Thanks to the capabilities of the Harrier, or in this case Sea Harrier, it enables equipment to be prepared and stored which, in a matter of a few hours, could multiply the number of oceangoing V/STOL bases. In the distant past similar schemes were studied for the conversion of merchant vessels into helicopter or even fixed-wing carriers, but the job always took weeks to months. Today, with such machines as the F-14, F/A-18 and E-2, such conversion is out of the question; indeed, the number of nations with seagoing fixed-wing airpower of the conventional kind has fallen to three (USA, France and Argentina) and will decline further during the current decade. In contrast, jet V/STOL technology has already put this kind of airpower aboard front-line ships of five nations (USA, Soviet Union, Spain, Britain and India), and others, probably led by Italy, will be added in the current decade. SCADS gives further impetus, in that for a relatively modest outlay a dozen other nations could almost overnight join the growing club of those with multirole seagoing airpower.

The advantages of a bolt-on system are obvious. In sudden emergencies there are never enough flight decks, and except for the US Navy the loss of a single one would be serious (in the case of two navies it would halve the number available, and in three others it would eliminate seagoing airpower entirely). With prestocked SCADS two, three or four more multirole V/STOL warships could be produced in a matter of hours.

The ideal starting point is a container ship, of 30,000 deadweight tonnage and capable of 25 knots (46km/h) in order to reach a trouble-spot quickly. In the form studied by British Aerospace the SCADS ship would become the operating base for six Sea Harriers and two Sea King helicopters, the latter being tasked primarily with AEW (airborne early warning). The ship is far more than a mere transporter of the aircraft; it provides every facility needed for their sustained operation for 30 days, as well as the ship's own defence system against air attack. In effect, it becomes a powerful warship, able to supplement the air defence and long-range attack capability of a task force or to serve as a convoy's outer defence perimeter.

To do the whole job takes about 230 ISO (International Standards Organization) containers, each 8ft×8ft×40ft (2·4m×2·4m×12m). Accompanying artwork shows how most of these would house aircraft fuel for the 30 day period,

SCADS ship layout

Below: SCADS (shipborne containerized air-defence system) is something that in the early 1980s is highly exciting, but it is almost certainly by no means the only bright idea to be triggered off by vectored thrust. This diagram shows how any modern container ship could be adapted so that, at less than 48h notice, it could be converted into an operating base for the world's most versatile combat aircraft. There are an unlimited number of ways in which Harriers and ships can be wedded, but SCADS appears in 1984 to be very hard to beat – whatever the budget!

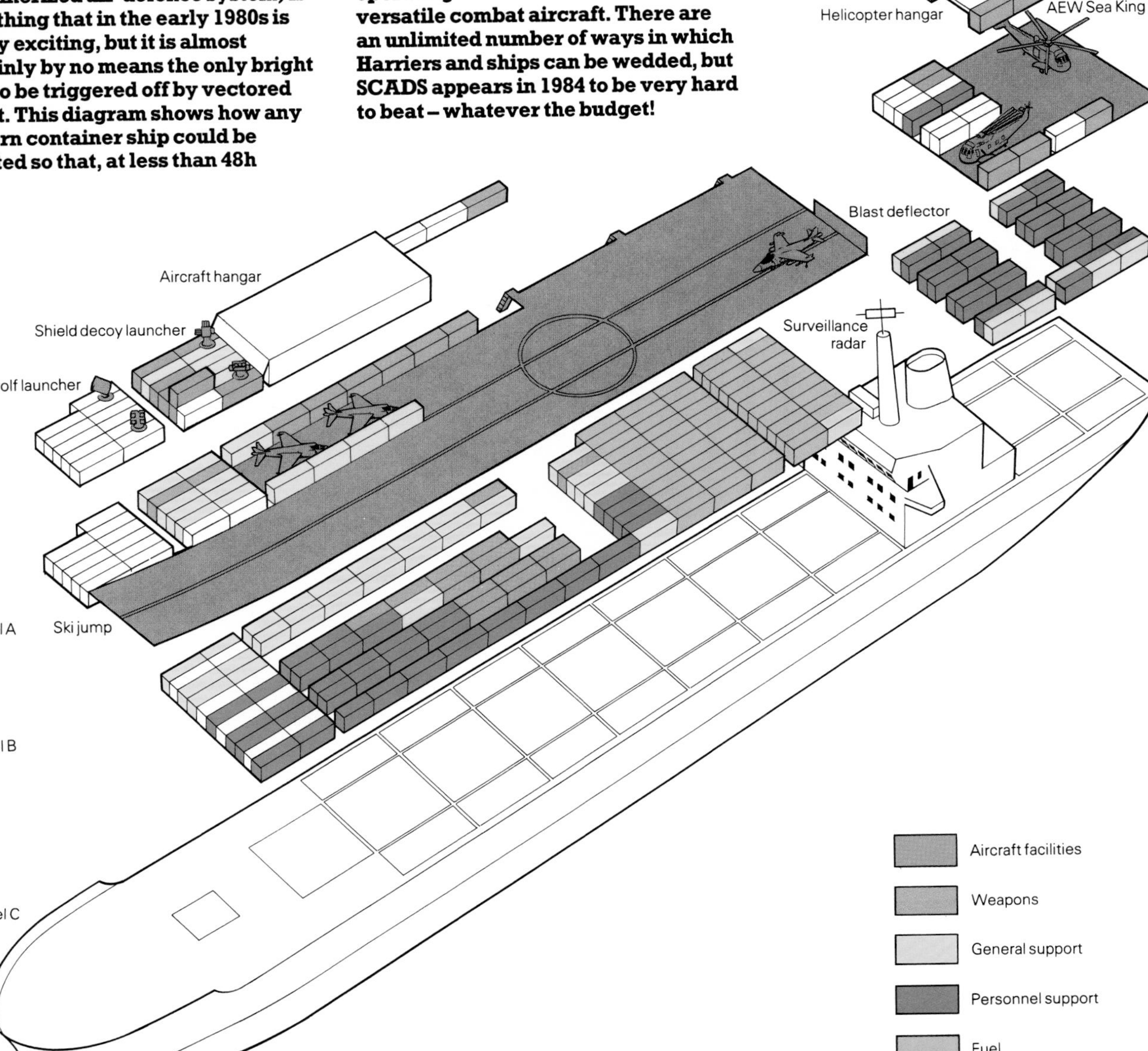

Right: Airpower en route to war: aboard the ill-fated *Atlantic Conveyor* in May 1982, showing the GR.3s (left) and 809 Sea Harriers. The SCADS system would turn such vessels into effective fighting ships in their own right.

assuming 50h flying per aircraft (a figure greatly exceeded during Operation Corporate). Others would be accommodation units and offices for the extra crew of some 190 men, while others would house drinking water, food, domestic/utility power supplies and other essential services. The operational side would have containers loaded with aircraft spares, workshops and test gear, aircraft ordnance, and a complete range of air defence systems including Seawolf missiles, their handling gear and (possibly vertical) launchers, surveillance and Seawolf direction radars, active countermeasures and passive/decoy systems (Shield is favoured). There would also be a flying control station, Plessey aircraft direction radar, homing and blind-landing aids and extra communications. Prefab sections would add the helicopter pad and MGB runway/ski jump.

All the evidence shows that with such a system established in service, and once fitted to a ship to find and eliminate snags, a containership could be at sea again as a multirole warship two days after entering the conversion port. Proof of several elements of SCADS was furnished by the *Atlantic Conveyor*, but of course that vessel was hastily converted as a mere V/STOL transporter and had no previously designed installations, no runway and no defences. At the time of writing, the Royal Navy is testing the RFA (Royal Fleet Auxiliary) *Reliant* in the South Atlantic, having converted her from the containership *Astronomer*, but with helicopters only. Clearly, the next step is to test a full V/STOL conversion.

Incidentally, the point must be made in this book that several almost off-the-cuff tests have shown that the AV-8A, and certainly the Sea Harrier, has a large potential in the ASW (anti-submarine warfare) role because of its high speed, versatile weapon capability (such as Stingray), agility and ability to hover. This is unlikely ever to be a primary role, but the Sea Harrier in particular could certainly add ASW to the missions it could perform in the SCADS method of deployment.

Skyhook in action

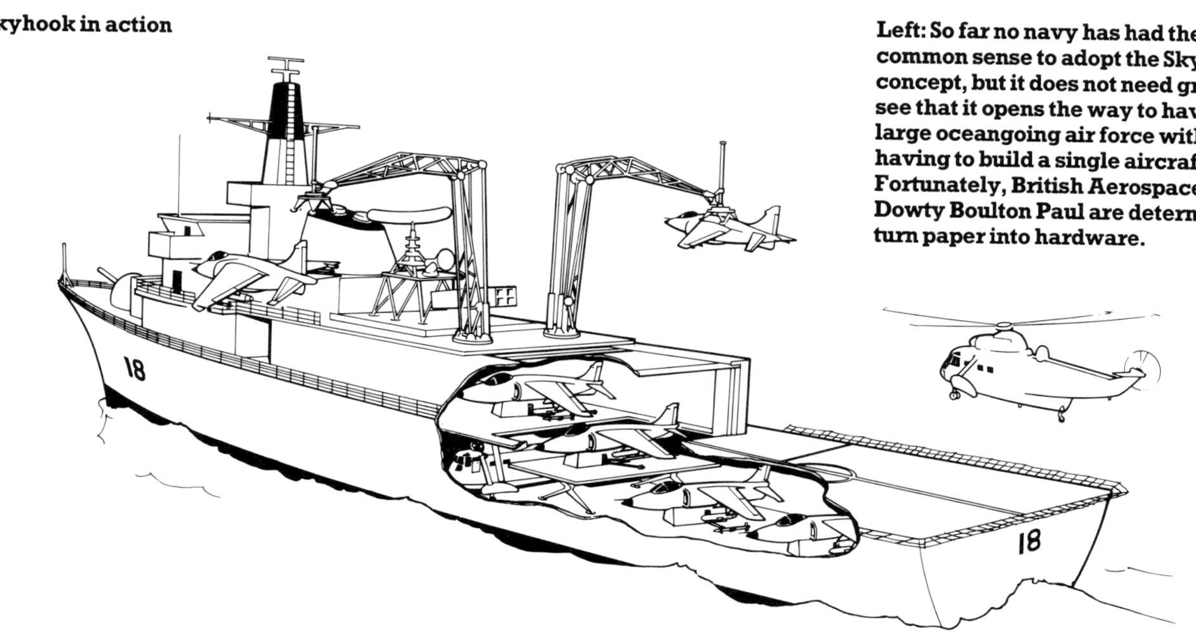

Left: So far no navy has had the common sense to adopt the Skyhook concept, but it does not need great IQ to see that it opens the way to having a large oceangoing air force without having to build a single aircraft carrier. Fortunately, British Aerospace and Dowty Boulton Paul are determined to turn paper into hardware.

The startling Skyhook

If SCADS will revolutionize a nation's rapidly available airpower at sea, Skyhook seems to border on science fiction, until one recalls that BAe have tried out its essential elements. In a nutshell it is a shipboard crane which reaches out and grabs a Harrier in the hover. Thereafter the aircraft can be refuelled and released; or it can be swung inboard and tucked into a parking slot below decks, all under precise control as if done by an extremely capable giant. At first glance it looks as if the ship merely swings out the jib of a crane fitted with a hook mechanism, but in fact the system is quite sophisticated.

British Aerospace has studied the design and operation of a Skyhook installation on a frigate, but of course it could be applied to any warship, or merchant vessel, of above about 5,000 tons displacement. In a typical frigate installation the Skyhook could form part of a standard package measuring 55ft×170ft ×18ft (16·8m×51·8m×5·5m) providing the total installation needed for the operation of four Sea Harriers and two Sea Kings, complete with below-decks hangar space and two Skyhook cranes.

To recover aboard a Skyhook ship the pilot uses only standard piloting techniques to make a decelerating transition and then to formate alongside at the speed of the ship. The Skyhook, extended from its normal stowed position on deck, is automatically controlled by ship motion sensors and hydraulic rams so that its pick-up head is space-stabilized; in other words, it moves ahead at the speed of the ship in a perfectly straight line no matter how the ship may heave and roll. Attached to the pick-up system is a day/night hover sight which, using two vertical lines and one horizontal line in one plane and two horizontal index markers nearer to the pilot, gives clear guidance information so that the pilot can move inboard to the correct distance from the ship, at the right height and correctly located fore-and-aft. The precision demanded is not onerous: the pilot merely has to maintain position within a box with 10ft (3m) sides, so an

Right: Sea Harrier FRS.1s recovering aboard *Hermes* in May 1982, with an RFA oiler and plane-guard Sea King in the background. At the time of writing no Sea Harrier has even been damaged in recovering aboard its ship.

The hover sight

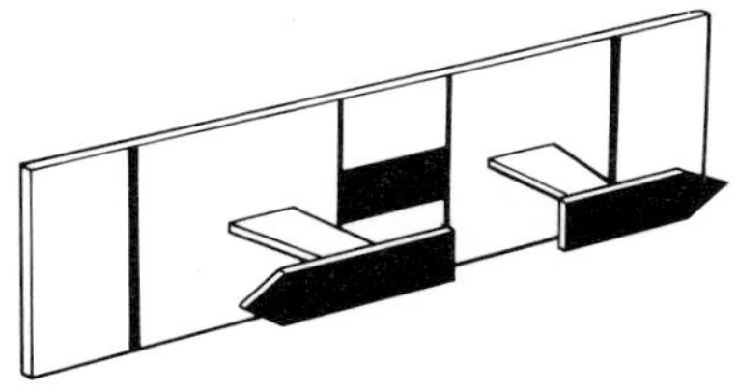

Below: A sequence showing how aircraft capture by the BAe-promoted Skyhook is envisaged. The guidance display – simplicity itself – is carried on the end of the Skyhook. It uses parallax to allow the pilot to formate his aircraft correctly in the contact window.

Too high; too distant; too far forward

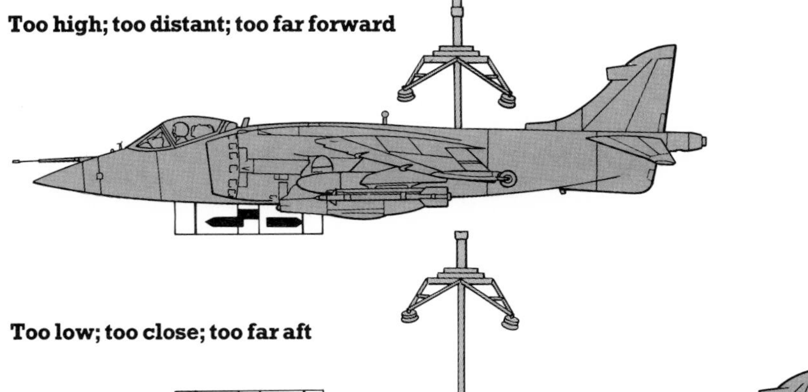

Too low; too close; too far aft

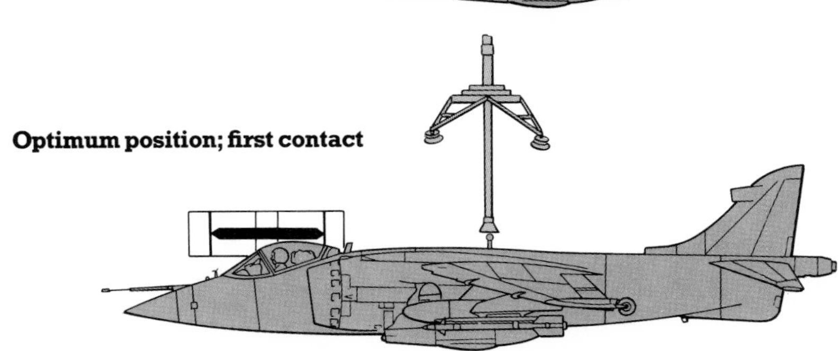

Optimum position; first contact

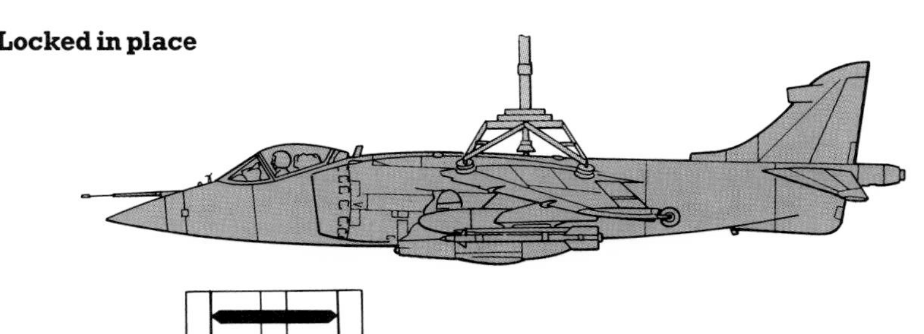

Locked in place

Left: If any of the local farmers around Dunsfold had been watching these early experiments in 1982 they might indeed have thought Kingston-Brough Division were mad. G-VTOL proved that, from the pilot's point of view, the Skyhook concept is "a piece of cake".

Skyhook is space-stabilised **Skyhook details**

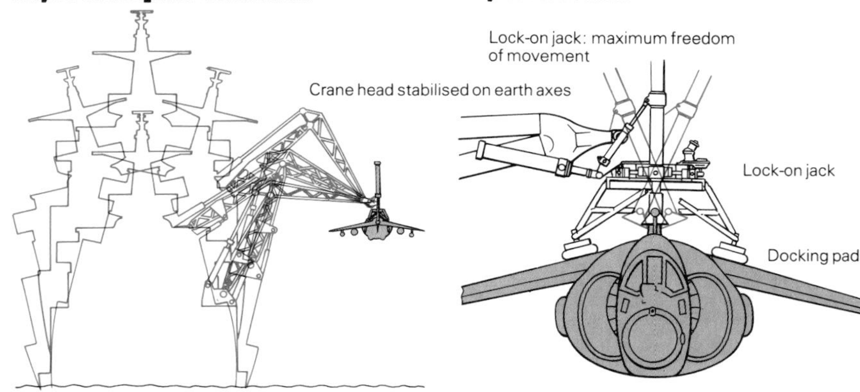

exhausted pilot with only basic training ought to have no great difficulty.

Once it is moving at the speed of the ship within the contact window (the 10ft cube) the Sea Harrier is acquired by an on-board optical system which looks down from the Skyhook and measures the exact angle and distance to a small pick-up probe extended above the aircraft. Tests have shown that there is no problem in automatically guiding the lock-on jack over the pick-up probe in an elapsed time of about one second, with the aircraft anywhere in the capture window. Lock-on is indicated to the pilot by a series of lights and/or by R/T. He at once slightly reduces power, putting load on the pick-up, and the jack simultaneously pulls the aircraft upwards firmly against the resilient docking pads. The capture is then complete, after a total time of only a few seconds.

For fluid replenishment the pilot stays aboard, with the engine at ground idle, while the fuel and water tanks are topped up. At 1,100lb (500kg)/min, this task takes 5 minutes or less. The existing sockets for these fluid systems could be used, with large articulated hose-arms, or, without much difficulty, the Sea Harrier could be provided with new fuel/water sockets close to the pick-up probe. Alternatively, for change of pilot or for rearming, the engine is shut down as soon as capture is complete and the Skyhook officer swings the aircraft inboard, the action automatically and progressively phasing out the space-stabilization. By the time the aircraft arrives inboard it is fully ship-stabilized, pitching and rolling with the ship. If the aircraft is needed for another sortie it is lowered through the deck access on to a trestle already pre-loaded with all the external stores needed. The latter are automatically elevated by powered crutches on to their ejector/release units, and the entire rearming can be automatic. Within the trestle the gun pods can be replaced by new pods with full magazines. Complete rearming takes just under ten minutes.

If the aircraft is not tasked with an immediate sortie it can be released from the Skyhook and then moved to its allotted parking space below deck. The trestle carrying the Sea Harrier is moved completely mechanically, under remote control, to the selected location. This calls for no sweating manpower, eliminates damage, is unaffected by the roughest of seas, and enables aircraft to be parked almost touching each other, and with great saving in time. Skyhook design has been based on a 4,000 ton ship and Sea State 6, which means conditions would be unacceptable for only about 1 per cent of the time on an averaged worldwide basis.

When an aircraft below decks is needed for a sortie, the hangar access is opened and the Skyhook programmed to lock-on to the aircraft. As soon as this is confirmed, the trestle releases the aircraft and the Skyhook swings the Sea Harrier outboard, at the same time changing to the space-stabilized mode. Meanwhile the pilot has been starting the engine and doing his cockpit checks, in telebrief contact with the ship. When his checks are complete, the pilot signals he is ready for takeoff. The jack slowly pushes the Sea Harrier down away from the pads, the pilot at once beginning to feel the need for small hovering flight control movements, while checking that the nozzles are at about 90°. He opens up to high power over a period of 10 seconds, taking load off the Skyhook jack until green lights flash on the lock-on board. The pilot then adds a trifle more power; as soon as the jack senses an up-load it disconnects and withdraws rapidly upwards. The pilot then rolls slightly away from the ship and begins an accelerating transition.

Obviously such a system could turn frigates and even destroyers into potent aircraft carriers. Something like it seems bound to come into increasingly wide use, despite its drawback in making all takeoffs VTO instead of STO. The latest Vosper escort carrier gets the best of both worlds by using a ski jump for takeoff and Skyhook for recovery. BAe has teamed up with Skyhook subcontractor Dowty Boulton Paul to search for a customer. Its importance is so inescapably great that in the course of time it is bound to happen. The Soviet Union has no inhibitions, and simply adopts good ideas when it sees them. It could well be that in that country the Skyhook will first go into mass production, though they have some catching-up to do.

The Super Harrier?

Even Skyhook does not exhaust the list of possible future methods of operating Harriers, but the remainder of this chapter must turn to future developments of the aircraft itself. Though it is unwise in aviation to suggest that an ultimate has ever been reached, the AV-8B looks close to the limit of what can be flown with today's Pegasus engine. The writer has long believed that a case could be made for a tandem-wing aircraft, which could probably have favourable jet-induced circulation round the wings (better than AV-8B) and would show advantages in compactness, agility and the ability to change the engine upwards without removing the wing. This is just one of several configurational possibilities, but – though there has never been a time in aviation when so many diverse configurations and propulsion arrangements presented themselves – this book is not about V/STOL but about the Harrier. Future possibilities are therefore confined to aircraft that can be regarded as Super Harriers.

Though there is still an unfortunate element in many countries, most notably in the United States, that continues to regard the Harrier concept as too limited or outdated to be worthy of consideration, in fact its simplicity has always been its greatest strength. Almost all the alternative V/STOL fighter schemes being proposed in the USA today would have made Sir Sydney Camm's hair stand on end. They would be not only astronomically expensive and trouble-ridden, but in a real war would undoubtedly impose a severe burden on supporting personnel and highly vulnerable to battle damage. Moreover, not one could join a combat unit within ten years, and if the XFV-12A is any guide, most will fall by the wayside.

It seems infinitely more sensible to start with a Harrier and see how it can be developed. Unlike the situation at the start of the AV-8B project, this time it is essential to seek further progress with the engine. For several years, 1969-82, virtually all Pegasus development was directed towards longer life, improved reliability and reduced costs. Now the emphasis is returning to climbing further up the thrust ladder, and there are two immediate paths to take. One is PCB (plenum-chamber burning), described later. The other is going on with the normal progression made with almost all gas turbines in increasing the mass flow, raising the gas temperature, improving component efficiencies, and tightening up clearances and improving seals throughout the engine to reduce air or gas leakage.

The immediate Pegasus prospect is the 11-21D, already bench tested, in which significantly improved HP turbine cooling can lead to either extended life or increased thrust, a typical compromise being 1,000h TBO at a rating of 22,000lb (9980kg). Planned as the engine of the AV-8B+, which could replace today's AV-8B on the line in about 1986, the Pegasus 11-35 introduces a rebladed fan which increases mass flow from 432lb (196kg)/s to 451lb (205kg)/s, with a 7 per cent increase in rpm. There are small modifications throughout the engine to cater for the increased pressures. This engine has been running since August 1981 and is rated at 23,200lb (10524kg), though it is installationally interchangeable with engines in current Harriers.

The importance of PCB

For the more distant future, later in the 1980s, the most important development is PCB (plenum-chamber burning). This is the burning of additional fuel in the plenum chamber between the fan and the front nozzles, and is precisely similar in principle to conventional afterburning in a jet pipe. The main difference is that in an afterburner the extra fuel is sprayed into very hot gas, much of whose oxygen has already been consumed. In the Pegasus plenum chamber the added fuel encounters relatively cool air with all its oxygen present, so the potential thrust gain is very large. Gains in thrust at the front nozzles of 100 per cent can readily be obtained, and as the front nozzles provide roughly half the thrust of the engine the overall boost in power is about 50 per cent.

PCB is an essential for any supersonic V/STOL. It was a feature of the BS. 100 engine for the P.1154, and this was preceded by PCB-boosted Pegasus research for the P.1150 in 1961. It is a pity that so many years have been wasted, though at company expense Rolls-Royce continued with small PCB investigations in the early 1970s, for the AV-16 and other Advanced Harrier projects, and eventually PCB tests began to pick up again in 1980, latterly with MoD funding. So far all the full-scale engine running has been done with one of the oldest and least-representative Pegasus engines, a Mk 2.

Basically there is nothing very clever about PCB. All that has to be added are fuel manifolds, an internal burner to hold the flame while imposing minimum pressure drop on the airflow, and variable-area nozzles. Almost the only significant factor complicating the design of a PCB system is that the flow turns corners while combustion is taking place, but prolonged testing has established a successful system. In 1962-64 this was tested in sea-level static conditions with the Pegasus 2 mounted upside-down on an open-air bed, so that with PCB in operation the hot luminous jets from the front nozzles pointed skywards, causing noise but not erosion or reingestion problems. As the programme is based at the MoD Proof and Experimental Establishment at Shoeburyness the PCB tests cause no noise nuisance.

Following basic calibration and performance measurement, the tests moved on to study behaviour with distorted inlet airflow and with varying water ingestion, simulating torrential rain or snow. Water flow was increased until it was a veritable Niagara, extinguishing combustion on one side and then, with water reduced, checking that the PCB was

Above: This Pegasus 2 was used for the first phase of sea-level tests at the MoD Proof and Experimental Establishment, Shoeburyness in 1981. The giant front nozzles do not represent a definitive design.

Below: The PCB rig at Shoeburyness during test operation. The water spray visible is to cool ground-based instrumentation during the initial running-up test phase. Note PCB flames visible in front nozzles.

immediately relit by the burner on the other side of the engine. Simulated high-altitude testing followed at the National Gas Turbine Establishment. The results enabled the temperature rise, and thus the thrust boost, to be increased for further testing which by 1983 had the engine mounted in a refurbished Harrier airframe slung from a large gantry at Shoeburyness. The main purpose of the 1984 testing is to study the interaction of the aircraft and ground when suspended at all heights up to over 50ft (15m), and with the aircraft and nozzles at various angles. Subjects studied included surface erosion and temperature and, especially, engine performance deterioration due to hot-gas reingestion and the effectiveness of various methods of minimising reingestion.

Problems of erosion, reingestion and FOD are much intensified by PCB, which multiplies gas velocity and temperature of the forward pair of jets. The difficulties looked intractable, but today Rolls-Royce say the entire technology is well advanced and solutions to all the problems are in sight. The high-altitude testing had to explore handling and relighting up to altitudes well over 60,000ft (18·3km) and over an extreme range of AOA, because PCB engines are likely to power extremely agile combat aircraft whose lives will by no means be restricted to treetop height. Like modern afterburners, PCB needs to be fully modulated, rather than an on/off system.

There is every indication that the preferred operating method for a PCB-boosted supersonic Harrier derivative will be STOVL. The high thrust will enhance acceleration in an STO, and there are ways of solving the increased problems of jet scrubbing, intense noise impingement on the fuselge skin and, especially, fuselage heating with the jets aft. The nozzle control system, at present rigidly linking all four nozzles in unison, may have to cater for the fact that the front nozzles may or may not have PCB in operation, with a consequent possible doubling of front-nozzle thrust. Again, there are ways of keeping the resultant thrust vector at the optimum angle and passing through the aircraft CG.

A supersonic Harrier

As accompanying curves show, PCB is a "must" for a supersonic V/STOL. Even with an inlet system more or less like a Harrier, Mach 1·6 can be seen at the tropopause at around 36,000ft (11km). With more complex sharp-lipped fully variable inlets Mach 2 could be achieved, but there seems little advantage in doing so. The one big change that will almost certainly be called for in a supersonic Harrier is that the engine must be a three-poster, the two rear nozzles being replaced by a single central reheat jetpipe. Vectoring jetpipes are not new, Rolls-Royce itself having done prolonged testing with the RB.153 in the 1960s which had a rear afterburner and 90° vectoring nozzle. The method of vectoring such a pipe is usually to insert a doubly tapered portion which can be rotated by an external power source. Such a pipe is called a "lobsterback".

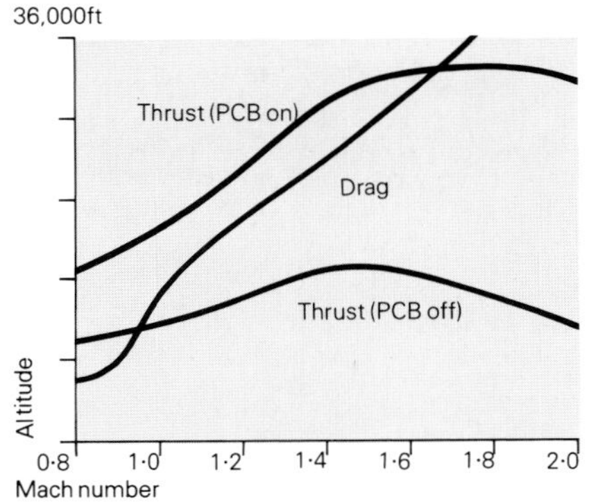

Above: Even the most generalized curves show that PCB makes an enormous difference to V/STOL aircraft performance at 36,000ft (11 800m). Though fuel burn is increased, as in normal afterburning, Mach number is doubled.

There are several advantages of the three-poster for a supersonic V/STOL. One is that it is possible to use an afterburner in the central rear nozzle. Another is that in cruising flight the flow through the engine is more direct than with four nozzles at the sides, and this is important at Mach numbers as high as 1·6. Most important of all, the installed drag is reduced and there are no projecting rear nozzles downstream; with PCB in action life would be hard for the rear nozzles of a four-poster engine. On the other hand, moving the front nozzles towards the underside of the fuselage and keeping the rear nozzles at the side has been shown to be practical. Front nozzles located diagonally downwards would send down PCB jets in the hovering mode which would strike each other above ground level and eliminate the hot fountain that results from two vertical front jets. This arrangement, with canted front nozzles and two rear side nozzles has been favoured by MCAIR in both the proposed AV-8SX and Model 279-3.

AV-8SX was a proposal dated 1981 by MCAIR and Rolls-Royce to gain experience with a rebuilt AV-8A. The PCB four-poster engine would be a Pegasus 11-03B initially, rated at 27,000lb, and later an 11-33B derived from today's 11-35 but with PCB to give a dry thrust of 24,500lb (12 247kg) and a maximum PCB rating of 34,000lb (15 422kg), in all cases in the static condition at sea level. The fuselage would be stretched, the inlets would be configured for Mach 1·6, and the wing would be of greater area but thinner, and fitted with larger flaps. The Model 279-3 is a study for a definitive supersonic V/STOL with the same four-poster PCB engine. Though clearly a Harrier descendant, it would hardly have one part in common, and the variable inlets and nozzles would have to be accepted as an inevitable surrender of the Harrier's present simplicity. With a 400ft (122m) STO the 279-3 could carry a weapon load of 18,000lb (8165kg), and a very large proportion of the airframe would be of lightweight composite construction.

Much depends on whether the customer accepts that the obvious way to recover to a land or seaborne base is by a VL. Almost all takeoffs would be an STO, but a landing at substantial forward speed poses all the difficulties of conventional fighter operation, which in wartime, with blasted bases and a lack of large decks, may just prove insuperable. Time and again it has been shown that it is safer to stop and then land than to land and then hope to stop. But even at light weight a VL could demand PCB, and it is to clear PCB engines in a landing at zero forward speed that much of the current research is directed.

Of course, both MCAIR and British Aerospace have countless proposls for other forms of future V/STOL. Some bear no relation to the Harrier at all, but most recognise the vital pioneering of the Harrier in establishing vectored thrust as the way that future land and sea fixed-wing airpower will surely go.

Tomorrow's V/STOL engine

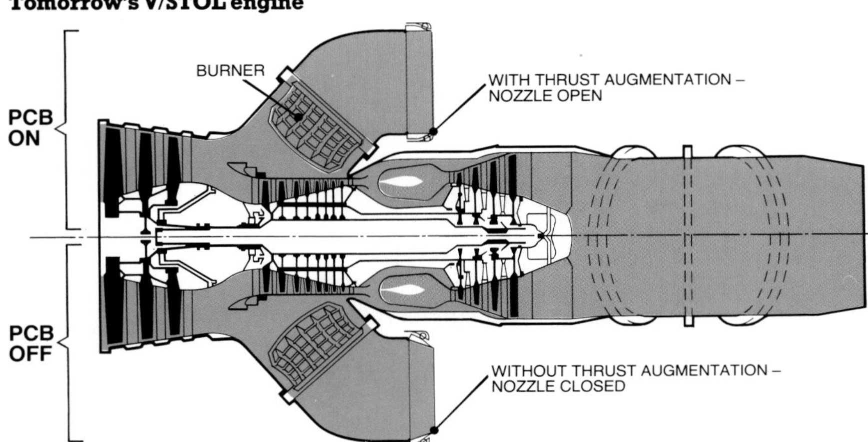

Above: This again is simplified, but the diagram shows the chief features of a three-nozzle STOVL vectored-thrust engine with PCB, such as will be needed for the highly supersonic combat aircraft of the 1990s.

Above left: Published by British Aerospace in 1983, this shows a possible appearance of a Royal Navy Sea Harrier after a mid-life update.

Left: Much less certain is the Model 279-3, envisaged by McDonnell Douglas as the preferred next generation after Harrier II. Powered by a PCB Pegasus, it could fly by 1990 if customers make up their minds this is sensible.

Abbreviations

AAA Anti-aircraft artillery
AAM Air-to-air missile
AAR Air-to-air refuelling
A&AEE Aeroplane and Armament Experimental Establishment, Boscombe Down
ACM Air-combat manoeuvring
ADC Air-data computer
AOA Angle of attack
APU Auxiliary power unit
ASI Airspeed indicator
ASM Air-to-surface missile
ASW Anti-submarine warfare
BAe British Aerospace plc
CAH Code for helicopter or V/STOL ship
CANA Argentine naval aviation
CAP Combat air patrol
CAS Chief of the Air Staff (UK)
CBU Cluster bomb unit
CCIP Continuously computed impact point
CCV Control-configured vehicle
CG Centre of gravity
CILOP Conversion in lieu of procurement
CNI Communications/navigation/identification
CWS Central warning system
DB Development batch
ECM Electronic countermeasures
EW Electronic warfare
FAA Argentine air force
FAC Forward air control
Finrae Ferranti inertial-navigation rapid alignment equipment
FOB Forward operating base
FOD Foreign-object damage
FRS Fighter/reconnaissance/strike
GR Ground-attack/reconnaissance
GTS Gas-turbine starter
hi High altitude, around 30,000ft (9·1km) or over
HP High pressure
HSA Hawker Siddeley Aviation Ltd
HUD Head-up display
IFF Identification friend or foe
IGV Inlet guide vane
INAS Inertial nav/attack system
INS Inertial nav system; Indian Navy Ship
IR Infra-red
IRCM IR countermeasures
LERX Leading-edge root extension
LGB Laser-guided bomb
LIDs Lift-improvement devices
lo At minimum safe level above ground
LP Low pressure
LRMTS Laser ranger and marked-target seeker
MAD Magnetic anomaly detection
MCAIR McDonnell Aircraft Co (also written McAir)
MCAS Marine Corps Air Station
MDC Miniature detonating cord
MEXE Military Engineering Experimental Establishment (now MVEE)
MFD Multifunction display
MIRLS Miniature infra-red line scanner
MOU Memorandum of understanding
MWDP Mutual Weapons Development Program
NAS Naval Air Station
NASA National Aeronautics and Space Administration
NATC Naval Air Test Center
NBC Nuclear/biological/chemical
Obogs On-board oxygen generating system
OCU Operational Conversion Unit
PCB Plenum-chamber burning
PoW Prisoner of war
PPI Plan-position indication
RAE Royal Aircraft Establishment
RAF Royal Air Force
RAT Ram-air turbine
RCV Reaction control valve
RDT&E Research, development, test and engineering
RN Royal Navy
RNAS RN Air Station
RVL Rolling vertical landing
RWR Radar warning receiver
SAAHS Stability-augmentation and attitude-hold system
SAM Surface-to-air missile
SL Sea level
SLEP Service life extension program
STO Short takeoff
STOVL STO/vertical landing
Tacan Tactical air navigation
TBO Time between overhauls
TDC Through-deck cruiser
TES Tripartite Evaluation Squadron
TEZ Total Exclusion Zone
TGP Twin-gyro platform
TO Takeoff
TRU Transformer/rectifier unit
TWS Track while scanning
UFC Up-front control
UHF Ultra-high frequency
USMC United States Marine Corps
Viff Vectoring in forward flight
VL Vertical landing
VMA Marine fixed-wing attack squadron
V/STOL Vertical or short takeoff and landing
VTO Vertical takeoff
WAC Weapon-aiming computer
WOD Wind over the deck

Specifications

	Harrier GR.3	Harrier T.4	Sea Harrier FRS.1	AV-8C	AV-8B/Harrier GR.5
Engine type	Pegasus 103	Pegasus 103	Pegasus 104	F402-RR-402	F402-RR-406/Pegasus 105
TO thrust (wet)	21,500lb (9752kg)	21,500lb (9752kg)	21,500lb (9752kg)	21,500lb (9752kg)	21,700lb (9843kg)
Span	25ft 3in (7·7m)	25ft 3in (7·7m)	25ft 3in (7·7m)	25ft 3in (7·7m)	30ft 4in (9·25m)
	29ft 8in (9·04m) with ferry tips				
Length	46ft 10in (14·27m)	55ft 9·5in (17·0m)	47ft 7in (14·5m)	45ft 7in (13·89m)	46ft 4in (14·12m)
Height	11ft 4in (3·5m)	13ft 8in (4·17m)	12ft 2in (3·71m)	11ft 4in (3·45m)	11ft 7·75in (3·53m)
Wing area	201·1sq ft (18·68m^2)	201·1sq ft (18·68m^2)	201·1sq ft (18·68m^2)	201·1sq ft (18·68m^2)	230sq ft (21·37m^2)
	216·0sq ft (20.1m^2) with ferry tips				
Fuel capacity	630gal (2865lit)	630gal (2865lit)	630gal (2865lit)	610gal (2775lit)	915gal (4163lit)
Basic op'g weight	12,640lb (5734kg)	13,440lb (6096kg)	12,990lb (5892kg)	12,565lb (5699kg)	12,922lb (5861kg)
Max TO weight	26,000lb (11794kg)	26,000lb (11794kg)	25,600lb (11612kg)	25,000lb (11340kg)	29,750lb (13494kg)
Max speed (SL)	735mph (1183km/h)	720mph (1159km/h)	740mph (1191km/h)	740mph (1191km/h)	668mph (1075km/h)
Dive limit	Mach 1·3	Mach 1·3	Mach 1·25	Mach 1+	Mach 0·93
Service ceiling	51,200ft (15·6km)	50,000ft (15·24km)	51,200ft (15·6km)	51,200ft (15·6km)	(Not disclosed)
Strike radius	230 miles (370km)	—	345 miles (555km) max	As GR.3	692 miles (1113km)
Ferry range	2,340 miles (3766km)	—	2,300 miles (3700km)	As GR.3	2,830 miles (4555km)

Notes: length for GR.3 with laser, for T.4 without; strike radius is 1,000ft (305m) STO without ski ramp, hi-lo-hi and with max bombload possible plus two tanks; ferry range is without inflight refuelling.

Harrier variants

RAF

P.1127 Original prototypes, XP831, XP836, XP972, XP976, XP980 and XP984, Pegasus 2 engine rated at 11,000lb, later 12,000lb.
Kestrel FGA.1 Development and evaluation aircraft, XS688-696, Pegasus 5 engine rated at 15,500lb. Equipped TES, six later shipped to USA as XV-6A, 64/18262-18267. Total 9.
P.1127(RAF) Also designated Harrier GR.1 DB (Development Batch), XV276-281, used for trials and other work by BAe, Rolls-Royce, A&AEE, RAE and other operators, Pegasus 6 rated at 19,000lb. Total 6.
Harrier GR.1 First production aircraft, XV738-762, XV776-810, XW630, XW763-770 and XW916-924 (last batch preceded 763-770). Pegasus 6 Mk 101 rated at 19,000lb. Equipped RAF No 233 OCU and Nos 1, 3, 4 and 20 Sqns. Total 78.
Harrier GR.1A Designation of GR.1 aircraft after conversion to Pegasus 10 Mk 102 engine rated at 20,500lb. Total 61.
Harrier T.2 Tandem-seat dual trainer with combat capability, two development aircraft XW174-175, and 12 production XW264-272 and XW925-927 (last two completed as T.2A). Pegasus 6 Mk 101.
Harrier Mk 52 Company demonstrator built approximately to T.2 standard but with strakes in lieu of gun pods, later re-engined with Mk 103 Pegasus, one aircraft variously G-VTOL or ZA250.
Harrier T.2A Designation of T.2 after conversion to Pegasus 10 Mk 102, total 9, plus XW926-927 completed to this standard.
Harrier GR.3 Designation of updated Harrier GR.1/1A re-engined with Pegasus 11 Mk 103 rated at 21,500lb, plus RWR and laser nose. Total 56 conversions, plus XZ128-139, XZ963-973, XZ987-999, an additional 36 built as GR.3 (RAF single-seat total 114).
Harrier T.4 Designation of T.2/2A aircraft after conversion to Pegasus 11 Mk 103, and most with RWR and laser nose. Total 10.
Harrier T.4A Two-seaters built with Mk 103 engine, XW933-934, XZ145-147, XZ445 and ZB600-603. Total 9.
Harrier GR.5 RAF version of Harrier II with Pegasus 11-21E Mk 105 engine rated at 21,700lb. Serials begin with ZD318-320. Total to be 60.

Royal Navy

Sea Harrier DB Development batch aircraft of new multirole RN single-seater with Pegasus 11 Mk 104 engine rated at 21,500lb, XZ438-440. Total 3.
Sea Harrier FRS.1 Production aircraft for Royal Navy, XZ450-460, XZ491-500, ZA174-177, ZA190-195, ZD578-582 and ZD607-615. Equip 800, 801, and 899 Sqns and previously 700A and 809 Sqns. Total 45.
Harrier T.4RN Two-seaters to T.4 standard for Royal Navy, ZB604-606. Total 3.

USA

Harrier Mk 50, AV-8A Original aircraft for US Marine Corps, first 10 delivered with F402-RR-401 (Mk 802) engine and retrofitted, all others with F402-RR-402 (Mk 803) engine. BuAer Nos 158384-158395, 158694-158711, 158948-158977, 159230-159259 and 159366-159377. Equip VMA(T)-203 and VMA-231, 513 and 542. Total of 102.
Harrier Mk 54, TAV-8A US Marine Corps two-seater, F402-402 engine, BuAer 159378-159385. Equip VMA(T)-203. Total 8.
AV-8C US designation of AV-8As rebuilt with numerous airframe, avionic and equipment improvements. Total 47.
YAV-8B Two AV-8B development aircraft rebuilt from last two of first batch of AV-8As, BuAer 158394-158395. Total 2.
AV-8B FSD Four full-scale development AV-8Bs to second-generation design, with F402-RR-404A engine rated at 21,700lb, BuAer 161396-161399. Total 4 plus 2 static test airframes.
AV-8B Pilot-production aircraft, F402-RR-406 (Pegasus 11-21E) engine rated at 22,000lb. BuAer 161573-161584. Total 12.
AV-8B Limited production, F402-RR-406 engine. BuAer 162068-162085. Total 18.
AV-8B Full production, F402-RR-406 initially, possibly a version of Pegasus 11F-35 later. Planned procurement 306.
TAV-8B Two-seater of new design for US Marine Corps, derived from AV-8B. Planned procurement 27.

Spain

Harrier Mks 50 and **55, VA-1 Matador** Single-seaters for Spanish Navy to AV-8A Mod standard, US designation AV-8S with BuAer Nos 159557-159562 (Mk 50) and 161174-161177 (Mk 55), equip Esc 008. Total 10.
Harrier Mks 54 and **58, VAE-1 Matador** Two-seaters for Spanish Navy to TAV-8A Mod standard, US designation TAV-8S with BuAer Nos 159563-159564 (Mk 54) and 161178 (Mk 58). Total 3.
Harrier II (Spain) Single-seaters to same standard of build as AV-8B for Spanish Navy, designation not yet allocated. Total 12.

India

Sea Harrier FRS Mk 51 Single-seaters completed close to FRS.1 standard for Indian Navy, 601-606, equip 300 Sqn. Total 6.
Harrier T. Mk 60 Two-seaters for Indian Navy to approximate T.4RN standard, Nos 621-622. Total 2.

Picture credits

The publishers would like to thank the following organizations who supplied illustrations for this book:

Aviation Photographs International: 37 (top), 45 (top), 47 (bottom)
British Aerospace: 1, 2 (middle), 4 (bottom), 6, 7, 8, 9, 10, 12 (bottom), 13, 14, 17, 18, 20, 22, 23, 24-5, 25, 27, 29 (bottom), 30-1, 32, 33 (middle), 34, 35 (bottom), 37 (bottom), 38, 40, 41 (bottom), 42 (top), 44, 46 (bottom), 58 (bottom), 59, 60, 61, 63 (middle)
Ferranti: 26 (bottom), 39 (bottom)
McDonnell Douglas Corporation: 2 (bottom), 21, 48, 49 (top), 52, 53, 54, 55, 56, 57, 58 (top), 63 (bottom)
Ministry of Defence, London: Endpapers, 3, 11 (bottom), 12 (top), 19, 26 (top), 28, 35 (top)
Pilot Press: 13 (profile), 15 (three-view), 23 (profiles), 28 (profiles), 34 (profiles), 39 (three-view), 48 (three-view), 50-1 (cutaway), 52 (three-view)
Rockwell International: 49 (bottom)
Rolls-Royce: 4 (top, middle), 5, 6-7 (top), 15, 17, 50, 62, 63 (engine)
RNAS, Yeovilton: 33 (top), 41 (top), 43, 45 (bottom)
Royal Navy, Fleet Photographic Unit: 42 (middle), 46 (top), 47 (top)
US Navy: 11 (top), 29 (top)